Reel LIVIN'

A Trout Whisperer's Adventures in Paradise

Warren McClenagan

TAG Publishing, LLC

2618 S. Lipscomb
Amarillo, TX 79109
806-373-0114
806-373-4004 fax

www.TAGPublishers.com
Copyright © 2009 Warren McClenagan

ISBN 13 - 9781934606193
ISBN 10 -1934606197

Library of Congress Control Number: 2009942904

Cover Artwork & Interior Artwork: Gerald Emerson www.emersonart.com.

Quantity discounts are available. Printed in the U.S.A.

Please contact us at: info@TAGpublishers.com

Reel LIVIN'

A Trout Whisperer's Adventures in Paradise

Warren McClenagan

DEDICATION

This book is affectionately dedicated to my mother, Rosalynn for the countless hours of Raggedy Ann and Andy, and to my father, Dean for sharing his paradise with me.

Then he led me back along the bank of the river, and I saw that both sides of the river were covered with trees. And he told me, "Wherever the water flows, life will flourish – great schools of fish… Where the river flows, life abounds, and fishermen will line the shore…" Ezekiel 4:7

Save us a good spot by the river, Dad.

ABOUT THE AUTHOR

Warren McClenagan was born and raised in Gruver, Texas. After earning a Masters of Divinity with Biblical Languages from Southwestern Baptist Theological Seminary, he served in various ministry positions for ten years. He now resides in Darrouzett, Texas where he is part owner of the family ranch, pitching in when he is not sneaking West to fish, or holed up chronicling the latest misadventures of the Brotherhood.

ACKNOWLEDGEMENTS

I would like to thank: My lovely wife, Marian, who brought home the bacon while I chased this dream, Megan and Catherine for reading the early stories and offering their advice and encouragement, Ryan for never letting us forget granddad's eccentricities, and Leroy and Gertrude Born for their generosity over the years.

I am also grateful to all the members of the Brotherhood of Dean for their contributions to the cause, especially: Bruce Ayres for being such a loyal fishing buddy to Dean and for his invaluable assistance in reconstructing the details of how it all began, "Cousin Barry" for being the first to give voice to Dean's pervasive influence in our family and for dragging me back to paradise when I was too numb with grief to care, and Brian and Ben for sharing the memories and filling in the blanks.

I would also like to thank Taylor Streit of Taos Anglers for recognizing the gift and for taking me under his "fin" by giving me a little space in *Man Vs Fish: The Fly Fisherman's Eternal Struggle*. Thanks to "Pennsylvania," (US Army, Company E, 1st Brigade, 23rd Infantry: Anchorage Alaska, 1960-62) for introducing Dean to fly-fishing. I am indebted to a host of friends, too numerous to name, who read the early drafts and insisted that I keep at it, and to Georgia Davidson for a sound foundation in English, lo those many years ago. Also thanks to the fellowship of NHCC for their loving support and encouragement.

I would like to thank Dee Burks and the gang at TAG Publishing for recognizing the possibilities and giving this book a chance as well as for their exceptional input and encouragement.

Finally, thanks to God for fielding all those desperate prayers I threw His way when it seemed that He and I were the only ones who thought this was worth doing.

CONTENTS

Chapter 1

The Evolution of Camping

Camping has become a relative term. Fifty years ago, the idea conjured up roughly the same image in the minds of all outdoorsmen: smoke inhalation from an open fire and back pain from sleeping on the ground. I was born at a time that has allowed me to experience the evolution of camping first hand—from a night out under the stars at a catfish pond in the Texas Panhandle to the relative comfort of a 32-foot travel trailer 9,500 feet up in the Rockies. Given the rate of change, we may not recognize what future generations call "camping."

The pursuit of comfort has been the motivating force behind most of the changes that have occurred among outdoor enthusiasts over the last century. From the beginning, however, the concepts of comfort and camping have proven to be strange bedfellows, and there exists an uneasy tension between the two. On some level, the original spirit of camping is incrementally compromised with every attempt to make the experience less vexing. In fact, there comes a point at which we may become so comfortable that we wonder whether the effort really qualifies as camping at all.

Don't these "improvements," when taken to extremes, have the unfortunate result of recreating, albeit in miniature, the very setting we are trying to escape? If this troubles you as a camper of the "old school," let me ease your mind with this truth: the camping gods will not be mocked. With every action intended to make the experience more pleasant, there is an equal and opposite reaction at work. This is the first law of camping dynamics. The effect is such that, no matter what advances are made, the original "pain in the ass" quotient (PIAQ) remains constant.

For example, one of the first attempts to domesticate the camping experience was the tent. Early designs were far too bulky and heavy to be of much use to anyone who wanted to get more than a few hundred feet into the wilderness. The employment of nylon and aluminum solved this problem. The modern, full-sized tent is housed in a nylon shell, complete with drawstring, and is about the size of a rolled up sleeping bag. Thus equipped, a new generation of campers took to the woods confident that we were one up on Mother Nature. The sensation was short-lived.

The tent is indeed quite portable...the first time you use

it. But only blind optimism can explain the naïveté that led us to overlook the mystery of how 50 square yards of fabric, 90 feet of tubing, and half a dozen 8-inch stakes could be compressed into such a small sack. Some crafty combination of vacuum packing and shrink-wrapping must be at work. The result is that the tent is not easily dislodged from its nylon cocoon, and, once out, can never be completely stuffed back in.

This fact rudely dawned upon me years ago as I watched my dad dance spastically about a gravel tent pad, cursing like a well-seasoned sailor, while failing to dislodge even one piece of his new tent from the iron clutches of its bag. This happened as we were setting up camp on the shores of Taylor Lake, near the headwaters of the Gunnison River during the first "You Bear! Shoo! Fall Fishing Extravaganza," as our annual trips came to be known. It should be noted that the term "extravaganza," is a reference to the production that went into our effort, not necessarily the result. If we gave our experiences a subtitle, it might be, "The 10 Most Beautiful Places to Lose Your Temper," as this was but the first of many valuable, if not altogether pleasant, lessons we would learn during our yearly adventures in the Rocky Mountains of New Mexico and Colorado over the next several years.

Dad's anger finally got the best of him, and he performed a Caesarean on the tent bag. The dance and accompanying stream of cursing became known as the "Son-of-a-Bitch Shuffle" and was regularly employed in a wide variety of situations at the McClenagan camp thereafter.

As it turned out, this was only the beginning of our troubles. Another characteristic of this type of tent is that the method of erection is nothing like Dad had encountered with any tent in the past. He had served in the army in Alaska and had put up many a tent, so my suggestion that we refer to the enclosed instructions was summarily dismissed with a tone indicating that he had taken this advice as a personal insult. As you might imagine, our erection of the tent was dysfunctional, and resulted in another SOB shuffle, complete with flying aluminum.

Feeling ashamed of the destruction he had wrought, Dad laboriously repaired the nylon tent bag with the creative application of duct tape and fishing line, which he always kept handy for vehicle repairs. However, when it was time to break camp, we folded the tent, and it wound up forming a roll that was 3 inches too long for the bag. Since the mood at the end of a trip is always fragile, I thought it best to leave well enough alone. Nevertheless, Dad was not about to be defeated, especially since he had sacrificed valuable fishing time in the mending of the bag. So out the tent came and we took another tack. The second effort resulted in a roll that was 3 inches too short, and thus too wide to cram into the bag.

Round Three.

This time, Dad had me lie on my side at one end of the flattened tent and roll toward the other in an attempt to push the air out. "How are we going to get the air out of the aluminum pipes," I joked aloud as I performed this awkward maneuver. I usually resort to humor when things get uncomfortable. However, comedy is all in the timing, and mine always seemed to be way off. Dad took this personally as well.

Dad was quite pleased when, with a little effort, we were able to jam the tent back into the sack, and, by his expression, I knew he was about to rub it in my face. It fell to me, at that moment, to point out the pile of aluminum pipes lying behind him. I noticed that my name was sprinkled throughout the lyrics of the subsequent SOB shuffle. After he caught his breath, we began trying to work each joint in one at a time. We managed to get the first two in by hand. On the third, we had to use our stake mallet. The fourth ripped a gaping hole in the side of the bag. By this time, the tent and its sack were no longer inanimate objects to Dad, but evil entities who must be beaten into submission—creatures from the dark side. I took cover beneath a concrete picnic table as he donated the tent, piece by piece, to the wilderness around us, in a ceremony of unbridled emotion and intensity that did not end until the last mangled length of aluminum tubing sank peacefully beneath the surface of the lake.

I've since realized that we are not the only campers who have suffered these kinds of trials. In fact, they say it happens to all guys at some time or another. I may not even be the only goofball who has body-rolled the air out of his tent—but I could be wrong about that.

An invention that promised to spare us the drawbacks of the full-sized tent, while further increasing our mobility, was the two-man pup tent. By the way, it only takes a couple of nights in the great outdoors to learn that most camping terms are misnomers and many are downright self contradicting. Consider the following: sleeping bag, campfire, flashlight, firewood, feeding trout, glowing coals—you get the idea. This is certainly true of the two-man pup tent.

The name would lead one to believe that this, the lightest and most portable of dwellings, could comfortably sleep two men. However, research has revealed that the term "man" was actually added late in development as a marketing ploy. The original description, "two-pup tent" more accurately reflects the capacity of these little jewels. Those of us who were gullible enough to be fooled by the name hit the trail with one tent for every two guys in the party and experienced what was first described by soldiers in the foxhole as "incidental violation." The intimacy forced upon two men in the first few hours in such confines often results in serious emotional scarring, the effects of which are far outside the parameters of this discussion. There are recovery groups specifically designed to help people cope with this type of trauma, but most outdoorsmen adhere to an understood "don't ask, don't tell" policy.

A second drawback of the pup tent involves ventilation, or lack thereof, to be precise. Most people are not aware of the relative humidity of human breath. Within a few minutes of closing the flap, the walls of the pup tent begin to bead with drops of condensation. In short order, the fabric sags under the weight of the moisture, which has the effect of further reducing the space within the already tight quarters. Once the walls have reached the saturation point, the slightest touch will precipitate a bountiful shower on any occupant secure enough in his sexuality to have fallen asleep. Moving away from the walls means moving closer to one's tent-mate, and forces you into the classic choice between intimacy and a cold shower. Ironically, men typically take to the woods as a way to escape having to make this frustrating choice back home.

At some point along the way, such discouraging trials lead most campers to fall prey to a common myth; the idea that their vehicle is really an RV waiting to be discovered. Typically, it happens like this: While loading or unloading a vehicle full of gear, the outdoorsman, in what he mistakes for a moment of acute mental clarity, realizes that the interior of his vehicle is comprised of several cubic feet of space that is going unused once he reaches the campsite. This prompts the exclamation, "Hey! I don't need a tent. I can just sleep in the car!"

The revelation dawns with a great deal of force, convincing our woodsman that he has stumbled on a truly novel concept that has eluded all other campers up to this point. I have never known anyone who was able to resist giving this a try. After all, when we were kids, we slept in the car all the time. I could sleep two hours standing on my head in the back window! Heck, even the most hopeless insomniac can fall asleep at the wheel! Nevertheless, I am obliged to tell you, though I doubt you will listen, that, for reasons that cannot be explained, even Rip Van Winkle could not get more than a wink of sleep in a stationary vehicle were he to go camping.

You can avoid this misstep in the evolution of camping if you will try this simple experiment. Next time you are fighting falling asleep behind the wheel, pull over to the shoulder, or preferably into a rest area, shut off the engine, recline your seat to what you feel is a comfortable angle, and close your eyes. You will notice that the drowsiness that plagued you only seconds before has been replaced by a keen sense of alertness. Not only will you hear cars coming from miles away, you will hear bird wings, scurrying bugs, the breeze in the grass, cottontails hopping, and any number of other sounds that are outside the range of human hearing under normal circumstances.

Now dig around for something that can be used as a makeshift pillow and turn on your side. You will note immediately that, while your back bends easily along one plane, it does not bend comfortably side to side, even at the slightest of angles. If you are stubborn enough to continue, take your pillow and climb into the back seat where you can lie flat. That protrusion you feel between your third and fourth rib is the seat belt buckle. There are two of them back there, by the way, and they are arranged in such a way that you cannot avoid them no matter what contorted pose you assume.

When you are convinced that you must not have been as

sleepy as you thought, you may return to the driver's seat and continue your journey. One last piece of advice: look carefully both ways before you pull onto the road, because as soon as your tires cross the shoulder stripe, you will fall into a peaceful slumber. Since you are only going a few miles per hour at this point, you may well roll smoothly to a stop in yonder ditch and get your nap after all. One night of experimentation with the "my car is an RV" myth is sufficient for all but the most stubborn campers. It took two nights for me.

When the urge to go trout fishing became unbearable, and we did not have time to make it all the way to the mountains, we usually wound up on the banks of Clayton Lake in eastern New Mexico. Such was the case one crisp fall evening as I settled atop the toolbox that rested across the bed of my dad's pickup.

My brother, Brian, and Dad had chosen to share the cab of the truck, and thought they were getting the prime suite. What they did not know was that I had an air mattress and was going to beat the odds at last. I spent the better part of an hour puffing on the nozzle that refused to accept more than a mouthful of air at a time—and then only if I gripped the valve, just so, between my teeth, and blew with all my might.

This task led to several bouts of lightheadedness, which caused me to stumble around helplessly in the bed of the truck. My fellow campers found this quite humorous and added play-by-play from their vantage point in the cab:

"Uh oh, he's going over the tailgate!"
"Look out!"
"He's tangled up in the jumper cables!"
"Don't step on those...oh...potato chips."
"Watch out! That wasn't your fly rod, was it?"
"Look! He's got a Muddler Minnow stuck in his foot."

"Don't stub you toe on that… OH! That had to hurt!"
"Watch that pail of liver! Oh, too late."

No camper should take to the outdoors without the understanding that teasing and mockery are considered critical survival skills and are directed at anyone struggling with any sort of inconvenience or discomfort. This has the effect of creating a sense of relative comfort for the mockers, and sometimes, relative comfort is all you can get. This is understood by experienced campers, and we generally absorb such chiding in good humor, knowing that we may be on the other end of things next time.

The scratches on Dad's elbows reminded me that it had only been a few hours since I had been paralyzed by laughter at his expense. As I stumbled around that evening, I dutifully accepted my place in the scheme of things. Besides, I had tried to sleep in a pickup before and, as I settled into my sleeping bag at last, atop my cushioned mattress, I expected I would have the last laugh.

Just as my eyelids began to flutter, though, I felt my left hip touch the toolbox. In denial of the obvious, I turned on my back, thus redistributing my weight to compensate for the deflation that was occurring. "Perhaps," I thought, "the warm air in the mattress is merely condensing as it cools." Within another minute, I felt my shoulders touch down, followed in a matter of seconds by my buttocks. By lying very rigid, I bought myself a paltry 15 seconds.

I blew the mattress up again a couple of times, thinking that if I could beat the leak to sleep, I might win after all. In the end, I had to admit to myself that I was fighting a losing battle. In keeping with the first law of camping dynamics, the time it takes for an air mattress to deflate is equal to the time it takes the user to fall asleep—minus three seconds. My only consolation was that I was awake to witness a raccoon slipping into the pickup bed and making short work of Brian's stash of Twinkies. Brian seemed to be sleeping peacefully, so I decided not to wake him. And, by the way, you may add "air mattress" to the list of camping misnomers.

People with no experience in the great outdoors might wonder how three grown men could embark on an overnight camping trip with no plans for accommodation, save the confines of a single-cab work truck. The lack of sleeping space seems like something one might take into consideration before dusk of the first night out. Actually, this kind of oversight is common among those who succumb to the siren song of the wilderness. The lure of getting "back to nature" has the effect of robbing the camper of whatever shred of reason he or she may possess. All sorts of unrealistic and preposterous ideas are liable to be entertained as the glorious moment of departure creeps nearer. Here are a few I have heard or thought myself:

- "Yes, there has been a lot of bear trouble at that campground. That's why I have my pocket knife."

- "Map? We don't need a map. The brochure says you can't miss it."

- "Sure, 60 pounds in a backpack sounds like a lot of weight to lug uphill at 11,000 feet, but I'm not worried. I got the fighting heart award in football 25 years ago."

- "These modern boots don't really require breaking-in."

- "The Indians didn't have matches."

- "We won't need to carry much food since this is a fishing trip."

- "The Indians got along just fine without toilet

paper."
• "My wife will be so glad to see me when I get home."
• "I bet we are the first people ever to fish here!"
• "The Indians drank the water."

This phenomenon accounts for one of the most common phrases heard among campers, "Next time we'll have to remember..." Of course, no one ever thinks to bring a pen to write these things down. Why would we? The Indians didn't even have a written language!

According to the theory of evolution, only the fittest survive. In the evolution of camping, however, observation has led me to believe that a few of the "less fit" are left in the gene pool to entertain the gods with their antics – they are the ones laying in the seat of an old truck trying to get some sleep while swearing they are cutting the seatbelts out come sunrise.

Chapter 2

Popping Up

By the time the next trip rolled around, Dad was quite excited to announce that he had gotten his hands on a used pop-up. The pop-up is really a hybrid between the tent and its evolutionary replacement, the camper. You might think of it as a tent with a chassis. As you may have guessed by now, the name "pop-up" is somewhat misleading.

The vintage pop-up—which is, of course, what Dad found—could more accurately be described as a "crank-up."

This little gem is towed in its compact form and, upon arrival, is winched to its full height by a complex system of cables and pulleys hidden beneath the floor and in the walls. These cables suspend the hard roof a comfortable seven feet above the floor…if you're lucky.

If one of the cables should break—they were 30 years old the first time we used them—one of the four corners is then unsupported and its weight is thus distributed among the three remaining cables. We learned that the time it takes a cable to fail decreases exponentially with the failure of each preceding cable. The end result is what is known as a "pop-down." This occasional, but inevitable occurrence is part of what helps the pop-up maintain its PIAQ—and it kept Dad, who was somewhat tightly wound anyway, on pins and needles. If he was quick, he could get to the crank handle, which was mounted outside on the hitch, in time to get his knuckles and one kneecap busted by the violent spinning action of the pop-down effect. I usually chose to remain entombed within while he worked through his emotions.

The outdoorsman pursuing this level of comfort is forced to contend with maintenance issues that are not a part of tent camping. This might not seem worth mentioning if not for a phenomenon known as entropy. Webster's defines entropy as, "the general tendency of a system (the camper in this case, though it could be applied to the occupants as well) to move from a state of order to a state of disorder." What this means to the owner is that much of what worked just fine at the end the last trip will mysteriously cease to function before or during the next. This fact has birthed a popular camping maxim: "He is the wise camper who owneth not his own, but befriendeth the poor sap who doth." The same is true of boats, by the way, but that's another story.

Ownership has other drawbacks as well. For reasons not

entirely clear to me, some members of the family—read: wives—do not seem to appreciate the value of the camper as a landscape specimen in close proximity to the house, even when it is adorned with a coat of camouflage paint or a nice garden mural. As a result, our pop-up was stored in a Quonset barn out on the family farm.

Of course, the whole concept of the barn is based on the need to protect our "valuables"—I am using the term loosely here—from the elements. Some are surprised to discover that the rate of entropy in a barn is actually two to four times faster than what is experienced with outdoor storage. This unfortunate fact is largely owed to the presence of mice that chew out of boredom, pack rats that rarely make trades favoring the camper, and birds that are in constant need of nesting material and are prone to defecate on take-off. These three creatures formed an axis of evil against which my dad waged a dogged and heroic war. He eventually lost, despite the creative use of every means at his disposal.

Loud cursing along with the slinging of whatever objects might be at hand had only a temporary effect on the various vermin and required a great deal of energy to maintain. Small arms fire was also effective, but demanded a constant vigil, and resulted in a number of unsightly perforations in the tin roof of the barn, which belonged to my grandfather. He had never hidden his opinions about the folly of fishing and camping anyway, and did not need any more fodder for his displeasure, especially a bunch of bullet holes in the roof of his barn!

Inflatable predators, such as the snakes and owls dangling from the rafters, were supposed to strike mortal fear into the troublesome critters according to the salesman at the farm store. Apparently, however, they are not nearly so scary once they are covered with bird droppings.

When Dad showed me the plans for converting his paint sprayer into a motion-activated flamethrower, I suggested mothballs as a less apocalyptic approach; not that I have anything against the smell of napalm in the morning. We were never sure how much impact the mothballs had, but we grew quite fond of the sense of euphoria we experienced every trip during the first few hours in the camper.

On days that were too cold, or too nice, to work—the older Dad got, the finer the line between the two became—Dad feverishly employed himself repairing and improving what soon became our little castle on wheels. This is a classic pastime among campers since it serves as a way to pre-enjoy the adventures to come. This is an important part of the process since these outings are sometimes more fun to dream about and look back on than they are to experience.

On each visit to the Quonset, I was treated to a "tour" of the pop-up, each amendment being noted and discussed at length. Particular emphasis was placed on the impact each adjustment would have on our next trip. Space is always an issue in the pop-up, so the toilet, which sat in the middle of the floor and offered no provision for privacy, was dispensed with early on. Besides, Dad had bought the camper from his buddy Leon, and no amount of mental scrubbing seemed to the remove the unsavory image that thus clung to the toilet.

The addition of PVC shelving that could be broken down between trips was lauded as nothing less than pure genius. Every form of goop, glue, and tape known to man was employed to get the rotting canvas through each successive season. Of course, major changes sometimes necessitated a "trial run" to work out any kinks. Though rare and judiciously executed, these outings were invariably resented by our "critics"—again, read: wives—as "just another excuse to go fishing." Every outdoorsman must learn to stand boldly in the face of this kind of withering fire.

As the time for departure neared each year, the maintenance pace would gradually increase toward a pitched frenzy that usually occurred around midnight of the day after we had planned to leave since delays plagued our every step. There were wheel bearings to be packed, whatever that means, tires to be checked, and finally just prior to roll out, there was the annual ritual known as "the testing of the trailer lights."

Wiring is a favorite target of mice and is therefore most susceptible to sabotage. By this point in the process, we tended to be a bit anxious and tempers, never long among McClenagan men, were even shorter than usual. In keeping with the established pecking order, I was assigned to the driver's seat while Dad monitored the lights.

Dad: Okay. Push on the brakes.
Me: Okay.
Dad: I said push on the brakes!
Me: I am!
Dad: Well, nothing's happening. Are you sure you are on the brakes?
Me: I think I know what a brake is! Maybe you have to have the key on.
Dad: What? (Dad's hearing began to fade under stress)
Me: Do you have to have the key on to make the lights work?
Dad: Well, good night! Of course you have to have the key on!
Me: Okay.

Dad: Now, push on the brake.

Me: I am!

Dad: Well, push harder!

Me: I don't think that's the problem.

Dad: Don't tell me what the problem is! When you plugged in the lights, did you make sure the prongs lined up?

Me: Plugged in the lights? I thought you did that.

At this point, we met between the trailer and the pickup to plug in the lights, and to establish which party was to blame for yet another unforgivable delay. Blame, it turns out, is determined by pecking order. The first mutterings of profanity began as we returned to our respective positions.

Dad: Okay. Try it again.

Me: Okay.

Dad: No, damn it! Not the hazards! The brakes!

Me: I didn't touch the hazards. Those are the brakes!

Dad: *&*^&^%, the hazards are blinking! Try the blinker.

Me: Which one?

Dad: Hell, it doesn't matter! The left.

Me: Would that be your left or mine

Dad: %$&^&^%%$, Just turn on a blinker! Good, the left one works.

Me: Uhh, that should be the right one.

Dad: Son of a bitchin' mice, scrawny assed little shits. Next year…%$^$^%$%$.

Me: Maybe we can just remember to blink in the opposite direction that we are turning and put on the hazards every time we brake?

Dad: What? &^%^&%^, *&^&^%^%, $#@^^%%%!

We met again at the hitch to work out the wiring problem, after a heated and vocal search for a flashlight, wire pliers, and electrical tape. I, of course, was the bearer of the light, and Dad the electrical engineer. Light casting is an important, but somewhat boring task, and often triggered my attention deficit disorder. The result was that the light tended to drift off target regularly while I thought about how I might use the excess wire insulation in my new damsel fly pattern, or discreetly collected copper shreds that were just the right diameter for #20-22 Hare's ear nymphs. I was regularly brought back on task with a sharp reprimand.

Naturally, we began with the assumption that the wiring connections had originally been based on some color scheme. Unfortunately, that scheme had been complicated by years of tinkering with both the trailer and the pickup wiring, such that a certain amount of educated guessing was required: "Blue is closer to black than it is to white, so any excess blues (we were always fraught with an excess of blues) must connect to a black. Orange is really just a lighter shade of red, so they must go together. The striped wire does not reach, so it must not be necessary. Cap it off…" After about half an hour, we were back at our stations for another test.

Dad: Okay, push on the brakes.
Me: Okay.
Dad: I said push on the brakes! Those are the reverse lights.
Me: No, those are the brakes. Hey, do you smell something burning?
Dad: What?
Me: Do you smell something burning?
Dad: What the!!! ^%^$% ^%$%$ #$@#@ *(* ^%$!!!

By this time, little curls of white smoke were wafting out

from the sides of the camper. The meltdown of the insulation on the shorted wires was followed quickly by a meltdown from Dad as he sprang into action in a vain attempt to stave off permanent damage. He cut the corner of the trailer a bit too sharp and caught the iron bumper with his shin, which sent him careening across the driveway. Unfortunately, his course was rudely interrupted by the basketball goal post, which he had built years earlier out of heavy pipe casing rooted four feet down in a bed of concrete. It replied with a resounding "Dong!" when contacted by wayward humans.

At this point, he moved into second stage cursing, retrieving from retirement some rare and colorful antique gems of profanity. This was not the monotonous, drab cursing of an amateur, but the kind of "turn the sky blue" quality stuff that few ever hear, much less know.

Profanity as an art form has taken a hit in recent years. With the popularization of the F-word, people no longer put much creative thought into their cursing, and everyone thinks they can do it. To put this in perspective, consider the following: I have a great uncle who, in an argument with his sister decades ago, referred to her as a "spit-polished, 14 carat, double-plated, gold-rimmed asshole." They just don't make'em like that anymore!

The way Dad could weave these lines together was nothing short of poetic—kind of a high plains haiku that reached its climax only when his fingers became one with the melting plastic of the connectors.

By this time, lights were switching on in the neighborhood houses, and we retreated indoors until the smoke cleared. On the next test, I would find some excuse to put him in the driver's seat, "Maybe I'm not doing it right." As the monitor, I would say whatever he needed to hear concerning the working of the lights, and we'd soon be on our way, PIAQ intact. Whoever said that honesty is the best policy had never been camping with my dad.

Chapter 3

The Siren Song of Paradise

"Now boys, this is livin'!" When these words fell from my father's lips, no one in our family had any doubt as to their reference. Dad spoke in snippets or not at all and this snippet packed a wallop because it was employed exclusively in reference to his supreme passion—fishing and camping in the mountains.

Dad was Dean to me. Throughout my life, people have asked why we three boys always called our parents by their first names instead of Mom and Dad. I can only assume that my mother

33

and father did not know they were supposed to start calling each other Mom and Dad after I was born, and I just followed their lead and called them by name. So, to me, and to my two younger brothers, Brian and Ben, our parents were and always will be referred to as Rosie (she prefers Rosalynn) and Dean. There are those who insist that this practice reflects a lack of respect on our part. I can only respond by assuring anyone who has this attitude that the names Rosie and Dean carry no less affection or respect from our lips than any of the standard titles given to parents.

Everyone has his or her own concept of paradise: a place where our fondest hopes and dreams are realized. Call it what you will, Dad simply called it "livin'". What specifically he meant by this term is difficult to put into words. He was referring, in general, to any time spent in the Rocky Mountains.

Dad reveled in the excitement of that first whiff of pungent spruce and juniper that signaled the transition from plains to mountains and the bite of the crisp thin air reminding him that every breath was a privilege. Add to that the brilliance of the azure blue sky forcing the eyelids into slits by day and the innumerable mass of stars blanketing the black canvas of sky by night and its as if he'd stepped back in time to a pristine wilderness. The wildlife seemed wilder and infinitely more interesting, and even the food tasted better the higher you climbed. A bologna sandwich at 8,000 feet still beats the chef's best at the fanciest restaurant.

This wanderlust was so pervasive and contagious during our childhood that we three boys would come to learn the points of the compass by first identifying west as the direction of Dad's personal paradise. From those lofty peaks, the call of the wild regularly beckoned us to escape our everyday life for a short respite and recharge.

Then, of course, there is the water. Everywhere you turn,

there is water! It is part of a man's nature to feel more at home near water, a primordial instinct, I suppose. The privilege of water is always at the forefront of the minds of those of us who were raised in the rural Texas Panhandle. If we had to depend on what fell from the sky, we would likely have let the Native American Tribes keep this desolate landscape. Until technology made it cost effective to drill down and tap into the spring water that bubbles up from the Ogallala aquifer, no one homesteaded more than a few miles from the nearest creek, and only a handful of those watersheds were consistent enough to depend on. The prospect of sharing those creeks with the Kiowa and Quahadi Comanches who hunted the buffalo in the area was something even the hardiest of pioneers thought twice about.

In the mountains, the water is alive—running and leaping, tumbling and dancing. This water speaks, sometimes thundering, sometimes whispering, and those who pause to listen are likely to become entranced by its song. Water in the mountain lakes and streams was a vital component to Dad's idea of "livin'" and a vast departure from his daily experience back in the panhandle where 30 mile per hour winds could scour the earth blasting the flesh of man and beast alike.

Beneath the surface of this clear mountain water, occasionally breaking through as if to taunt the land bound, are the trout. Ghostlike and mysterious, they seem to appear and disappear at will. That oblong rock or transparent shadow...stare at it for awhile, and it will often grow fins before your very eyes. Keep watching and it will undulate, gracefully slipping a few inches left and right in rhythm with a passing smorgasbord of insect life that, from above, remains invisible. For Dad, the elusive creatures that inhabit the living water became the embodiment of the freedom that he experienced and summed up with the simple term, "livin'!"

Trout are a baffling paradox of complicated simplicity. Literally pea-brained, they are able to frustrate even the wisest and most seasoned of predators. We can fly to the moon and back and split the atom, but there are no guarantees when it comes to a wily brown trout. With every fish that fought valiantly at the end of his line, Dad experienced a sense of satisfaction; the true prey of every lifelong fisherman, the glorious obsession of those whose minds cannot long be kept from the water, even when their feet cannot take them there.

It is impossible to quantify the impact of an event or choice that may seem insignificant at the time. Its effects ripple throughout a community and down through the years, affecting our lives and the lives of those around us in ways we could never have imagined. Such was the case with that very first trout my dad landed on the bank of some remote wilderness lake decades ago.

Dad was not the first to catch a trout, nor was the trout he landed anything that merited special recognition outside his circle. Hindsight, however, allows us the rare privilege of realizing the consequences of those few seconds, consequences that no one could have predicted. Anyone who had the good fortune of knowing Dad both before and after this event would tell you that his world was never quite the same. I see the magnitude of that moment in my dad's life only because I stand some 50 years this side of it and spend a great deal of time chasing that same elusive creature that he sought so many times.

My dad's love affair with fishing started young and stemmed from a very fragile string of circumstances and events, if you believe in that sort of thing. While my brothers and I were introduced to the love of fishing from my dad, he wasn't so lucky.

The Siren Song of Paradise

My granddad, Babe, as they affectionately called him, died in his early 30s, leaving his wife, Ona, to raise my dad, Dean, and his two younger sisters. Dean was seven at the time. Money was tight and vacations were rare and frugal. By the time Dean entered high school, the man who would become his father-in-law (I.W. Ayres) graciously offered to take him along on summer vacations.

There is a good chance that I.W., or Pa, as we grandchildren came to know him, was acting in response to what I'm sure was merely a polite suggestion from his eldest daughter, Rosalynn, who'd had her eye on Dean since junior high. In the early to mid-'50s, Pa's old blue Mercury ferried his family, plus Dean, on yearly trips into the Rocky Mountains of New Mexico and Colorado. These excursions typically followed a couple of months of summer plowing. Sitting on a cab-less tractor, eating dust propelled by blast furnace winds out of the southwest that rake the panhandle that time of year must have made those mountains look and feel like heaven on earth to Dean

The Ayres family turned out to be an emotional gold mine for Dean. Through them, he was introduced to the Rocky Mountains. Among them, he found not only Rosalynn—a pretty good catch in her own right, who would become his partner for life—but also Bruce, Rosie's younger brother. In Bruce, Dean discovered a kindred spirit who became every bit as intoxicated with the mountains and the trout in their lakes and streams as he did. In Bruce, Dean also found a fishing buddy who would become his partner in crime. The word "crime" is used deliberately here, because that is what trout fishing was soon to become in the eyes of the elder Ayres.

Pa soon came to rue the day he had taken these two boys west. He would spend much of the next six years of his life trying to keep the two, whom he employed, anchored to the family farm while they conspired and finagled ways to get back to the mountains for even the briefest chance to chase the silver ghosts that swam in their dreams. Even though Pa was able to spoil their plans and keep them around most of the time, he was never able to recapture their hearts and minds, which were forever drifting west, yin to the rivers' yang.

Back on the Ayres' farm, bitter labor unrest began to develop. Some parties will still become flush in the face when the feud is mentioned. The old adage, "blood is thicker than water," does not necessarily hold true if there are trout swimming in that water. Pa became a most stubborn roadblock to "livin'". To this day, his grandsons will often chide one another with the classic line he used on the two farm hands that would be fishermen.

When he caught them in an idle moment—Pa did not believe in idle moments, and never had one himself—he would say to them, "You boys are doin' a lot more talkin' than workin' and I know what you're talkin' about. You're talkin' about fishin'!" They were content to let him think that, since they were usually talking, in less than kind terms, about him. Pa had such a way of expressing his disgust when he spat out this line, that a bystander might have believed that the elder Ayres had caught them engaging in a mortal sin. In his mind, he had. Naturally, the two young men, when robbed of the opportunity to fish, turned to *Field and Stream* and *Outdoor Life* for some vicarious satisfaction, and to keep the pump primed for the next outing. They soon learned that these periodicals, if left in a farm truck, raised the hackles of farmer Ayres to new heights—the sentiment has been captured in a fly pattern called The Angry Pa—and they endured many a tongue-lashing for such indiscretions. These were delivered with every ounce of passion one might expect from a preacher who has caught his son with pornography.

Pa had come of age during the Great Depression, and in his thinking, legitimate interests and hobbies contributed to the farming enterprise, improved the homestead, or were capable of being profitable on their own. This mindset was at the root of his attitude toward fishing, and most other sports for that matter. Pa could be quite creative when it came to finding something to keep Bruce and Dean occupied. A passing shower or thunderstorm was no reason to get excited. It had to rain several inches to shut things down long enough to justify the six hour drive to New Mexico.

Of course, the very act of forbidding an activity among teenagers usually tends to make it that much more attractive to them. If Dad and Bruce were not hopelessly addicted to trout fishing to start with, the fact that Pa was opposed to it was certainly enough to push them over the edge. Since Pa held all the financial strings in an iron grip, the young fishermen had little in the way of leverage, except the fact that, in fishing, they knew they had a subject at hand that was sure to irritate I.W. at the mere mention of it. They wielded this weapon, the only one with which they could exact any measure of revenge for their deprivation, quite skillfully.

Chapter 4

A Brotherhood is Born

Dad graduated from high school in 1958. He and Rosie were married the following August. After a brief experiment with college, he joined the army and wound up serving in Alaska. While he could just as easily have been among those who were training for what would become a very "hot" war, his unit was preoccupied with the "cold" one, quite literally. They were part of a presence that regularly flexed it muscles to remind the Sovi-

41

ets that, while Alaska was conveniently located just a few miles to their east, it would be a costly place to try to build a beachhead into the United States if push came to shove.

Someone in dad's outfit introduced him to fly-fishing while he was there. If memory serves correctly, the fellow was from Pennsylvania—Allentown, perhaps. However, an exhaustive search of dad's army records has failed to produce the identity of this fellow. Dad always referred to his army buddies by their nicknames when he told his stories, which makes it very difficult to get a fix on who was who. Squirrely, Musty, Shaky-Mackey and Paunchy don't show up in any official documents.

Anyway, this fellow, we'll call him "Pennsylvania," introduced dad to fly-fishing, whetting his appetite with tales of experiences he'd had on the famed limestone streams of the eastern United States. Putting a fly rod in the hand of a young man who is stationed in Alaska and already passionate about fishing for trout has predictable and powerful consequences. It is not unlike throwing raw meat to a hungry lion. There was no turning back.

By the summer of 1961, it had been a year since I.W. and his wife, Mary, had seen their eldest daughter, and over two since they had seen Dean, of whom they had become quite fond, despite his unsavory hobby. I'm sure it did not take much coaxing to convince the Ayres' that they should come north for a visit.

Officially, the ALCAN Highway winds some 1,422 miles through Western Canada, connecting Dawson Creek, B.C., to Delta Junction, Alaska. When you consider that Dawson Creek is another 2,000 miles by car from Gruver, Texas, the scope of this undertaking seems incredible. A total of more than 3,400 miles.

A journey of that magnitude demanded the participation of every able-bodied, licensed driver in the family. This meant that Bruce, who had just finished his first semester at Hardin Simmons University in Abilene, had no choice but to come along. I'm sure, though, he would rather have been taking care of business back on the farm (or at least wanted Pa to think so). It's heartwarming when young folks step up and make those kinds of sacrifices for the good of the family. You just don't see it much these days and I'm sure Bruce forced himself to travel the entire trip without one mention of the 'T' word or fishing.

Dad's correspondence with Bruce over the previous two years may have greased the wheels a bit since he had made frequent mention of the incredible fishing opportunities that awaited anyone fortunate enough to wet a line in the great state of Alaska. So it was that on July 1, 1961, after the wheat crop was safely in the barn, the Ayres family loaded the trunk of Pa's '58 Ford, strapping what would not fit inside to the top, and headed north. Among the luggage, Bruce managed to stow, quite discreetly I'm sure, his rod and reel, just in case.

On the other end, there is no telling how much effort dad put into researching the "best bet" waters, given the limited time the two fishermen would have. Dad was to become notorious in our family for collecting brochures about every possible getaway destination when he was traveling. The first stop at any hotel for him was the ubiquitous display stand in the foyer advertising local attractions. His selection criteria were straightforward. Any foldout that had a picture of a lake, a stream, or a mountain vista was a must have. If there were pictures of trout in the ad, he would take two brochures, so he would have one to share with the next fishing buddy who dropped by.

After pouring over each to determine if the destination advertised seemed promising enough to warrant a visit, he "filed"— actually piled—the brochures in his bathroom cabinet where he kept all his most valuable possessions. Over the years, this collection became a veritable loose-leaf encyclopedia of fishing and camping possibilities that we consulted any time our thoughts turned west.

With Alaska spread out before them, and only two days free to fish, it must have been difficult to make a decision. No doubt, Dad consulted "Pennsylvania" and made judicious use of his then infant pamphlet collection. He may have even stolen away on a personal reconnaissance mission or two. When the day came, Pa dropped them off at the Lower Russian Lake trail head on the Kenai Peninsula. The timing of the trip put them on the river a few days too early for the second run of sockeye salmon. This was likely intentional, since these famous salmon runs naturally coincide with equally famous human runs. Bruce and Dad were not the type of fishermen that relished the thought of shoulder-to-shoulder mass communion stream side, even if that's where the bigger fish were taken.

To separate themselves from the day-fishermen, the pair hiked six miles up the Russian River, passing Dad's army pack back and forth between them, before setting up camp. Upon reflection, Dad would later conclude that their passion for fishing may have trumped their better judgment as they marched off into grizzly country armed with a machete and a .22 caliber trapper's pistol—just enough weaponry to piss off any bear they might encounter.

They spent two nights there camping and fishing for rainbow trout and Dolly Varden. The fish were plump and plucky, having made the best of the gourmet offerings that came with the first salmon run. I can almost hear Dad delivering his classic line as a reminder of just how fortunate they were, "Now Bruce, this is livin'!"

This experience finished what the earlier trips to the mountains of New Mexico and Colorado had started. Dad and Bruce walked out of the Alaska wilderness joined at the hip as fishing buddies. Bruce can still tell you the make and model of Dad's first fly reel, 45 years later. Thus was born what I have come to call "The Brotherhood of Dean."

Dad was discharged from the army in the winter of 1962. At least it was still winter in Alaska when he left in April. By then, it could have been any season in the panhandle of Texas. I can say with a high degree of certainty that it was windy in our hometown of Gruver. His return trip took him through Seattle—April is the overlap of the wet season and the rainy season there—where he paused long enough to purchase a seven foot Shakespeare Wonderod, a Pflueger Medalist fly reel, and a Brownie automatic camera. In a few days, he was back at work on the Ayres' farm, and the fishing feud continued where it had left off years before.

A sound source of information about when to fish where, and where not to fish when, in a given region, is often the difference between the thrill of victory and the agony of defeat when it comes to trout fishing. It soon became clear that under Pa's watchful eye, Bruce and Dad were not going to have much time to scout out productive waters. They were fortunate just to wet a line.

To insure that they got the most out of their moments of trout fishing bliss, they picked the brain of Allen Byers, the town barber. He had two critical advantages over the average trout fisherman. He was his own boss, and his children were grown and gone. This freedom allowed Mr. Byers to do a good bit of legwork, often quite arduous, all over northern New Mexico and southern Colorado. This, combined with the fact that he relished telling his fishing tales, made him the perfect go-to guy.

It was Allen Byers who put the two eager anglers on to Charette Lakes (pronounced "sharetee" by the locals, Dad and Bruce always called it "sharedda"). These lakes were formed by diverting water from Ocate Creek into two volcanic pockmarks atop a barren plateau a few miles southwest of Springer, New Mexico. Granted, these lakes lacked the ambience of most other trout waters in the state. There was not a single tree to be seen and the wind blew strong and constant. But what they lacked in atmosphere, they more than made up for in trout. The fish in these old craters had developed a temperament as rough as the lava rock over which they swam. What's more, at this altitude, the dining season was quite a bit longer than it was for trout a few miles west which meant these fish had the physique to back up their attitude.

The final ingredient to the lakes' productivity had to do with access, always a critical component. The last few miles of the road that snaked up the side of the plateau was unimproved dirt and notoriously difficult. Fortunately, for the fishermen, no one bothered to tend it, and it became virtually impassible after any precipitation. So prevalent was the problem that someone eventually left a caterpillar along the road so that anyone who got stuck could help themselves. The lake was everything Byers had said it was, according to Dad, who never tired of answering the question, "What was the fishing like at Charette before they paved the road?"

"The edge was all rock, so it was hard to find a place to stand," he would begin. "And we learned pretty quick that you had better have a firm foothold before you cast."

"Why was that so important?" I would ask as if I had never heard the story.

"Warren, I'm telling you," Dad would say as he moved the edge of his seat, "as soon as that spinner hit the water, WHAM!"

At this point, in homage to Byers, Dad would display the patented Byers' hook-up gesture. This involved placing the fist in front of the sternum and bouncing it in a casual rhythm, fingers poised to snap to an abrupt, quivering halt at the point in the story where the strike occurred. The upper body sprang to attention at the same moment in response to the simulated take. This action, in some impressionistic way, captures the essence of a strike in a way that every fisherman who has ever seen it can relate to.

"Warren, those fish would jerk you right off the rocks if you were not ready!" He'd conclude. "And it was that way every third or fourth cast! Boy if I ever get my hands on the Son-of-a-bitch that paved that road…"

Much has changed since that fateful trip when Bruce and Dad bushwhacked their way up the Russian River with a couple of bed rolls, a can of beans, and a few potatoes between them. They cooked their "meals" in a gallon tin that they converted into an oven. Things are not quite so simple these days, but the passion lives on in the people whom Dean and Bruce have introduced to the Rocky Mountains and graciously included in The Brotherhood of Dean.

Chapter 5

Reel Livin'

An hour of driving northwest from Springer, New Mexico, puts a fisherman on the banks of the Cimarron River. For Dad and Bruce, this is where the real livin' began again. Cimarron Canyon is the northeastern gateway to the Sangre de Cristo Mountains. This is the first opportunity a panhandle fisherman has to fish for trout in running water.

Climbing from an altitude of 6,400 feet in the town of Cimarron to nearly 9,000 feet at the pass that overlooks Eagle Nest Lake from which the river flows, one gets the first real taste of the mountains that have been rising slowly from the horizon for the last couple of hours. The worse you need to get there, the slower these mountains seem to rise, appearing first as something that might be mistaken for a hazy mirage, then a bank of dark clouds. Once you exit the interstate and turn back toward the west a few miles north of Springer, the mountains march out to meet you. Soon after leaving Cimarron, you are swallowed up, neck deep in paradise.

Cimarron is a Spanish word meaning "wild and unruly." It's no coincidence that this describes many of the citizens who settled in the area in the early 19th century. Some found, in the canyon, a place where they could hole up when their nefarious activities out on the plains attracted too much attention from the law. Finding a place to hide out in the flatland complicated matters for people whose lives were already challenging enough. If someone spotted you on the high plains, it might take a day of riding just to get out of sight! Settlers were often lured to the plains with the promise that, once there, you could see forever. I suppose that sounded attractive to anyone in the Appalachians who had a touch of claustrophobia. But there is a catch. It is best illustrated by a conversation overheard between a husband, who had been touting the glory of the plains, and his wife, whom he finally wrangled into making a trip.

"See Honey!" He gleefully pointed out, "You really can see forever out here!"

"Yes you can," she responded, with a tone of chronic disappointment—the tone common to her gender after about a year of marriage, give or take—"but there is nothing to see!"

The St. James Hotel in Cimarron, now a National Historical Landmark, has memorialized the presence of those who found sanctuary in and around the rugged walls of Cimarron Canyon. Notorious gunslinger Clay Allison put down a local troublemaker who came into the hotel saloon looking for a fight. Frank and Jesse James also spent time there. Black Jack Ketchum lost his head there at the end of a noose.

By extension, the term Cimarron was eventually co-opted to refer to runaway slaves. Unfortunately for Dad and Bruce, the Emancipation Proclamation did not contain any clause concerning the liberation of sons or sons-in-law indentured to the family farm. In a sense, they led a new generation of "outlaws, wild and unruly," up into that alpine sanctuary. One can imagine the pensive looks they cast over their shoulders as they made their escape(s), echoing the sentiment of those desperados of the 19th century, "If we can just make Cimarron Canyon by nightfall, we'll be home free!" If you sit on the corner at the junction of Highways 64 and 58 in the town of Cimarron during July and August, and study the faces of those travelers who have Texas plates and turn west there, you will most likely recognize this same sense of desperate flight in their expressions.

Armed with unflagging passion, and solid information, all Bruce and Dad needed was permission. This proved hard to come by. One legitimate chance to escape the Ayres' farm occurred when rain made farming impossible. Even then, there were barns to be swept, machinery to repair, and, if nothing else, bolts to be sorted—oh the multifaceted joys of farming!

One incident in particular captures the tension that this fishing feud created between the employer and his employees. In the summer of '62, smack dab in the middle of wheat harvest, an unusually heavy downpour brought everything to a grinding halt.

Over four inches of rain meant that the combine would not be able to get into the field for several days because of the mud. Barns were swept, machinery was repaired, and bolts were sorted. But, much to Pa's dismay, it looked like they were still several days from being able to cut wheat. After employing the last of his stall tactics, Pa begrudgingly stepped out of the way as Dad and Bruce tossed their equipment into Dad's '56 Chevy; they were off in a flash. Experience had taught them to keep their gear at the ready since any dallying on their part gave Pa extra time to reconsider and perhaps think of some needless task that would delay them for hours if not days.

They left Pa fussing about not being able to get into the field while fuming that Dad and Bruce had been able to get away to waste their time so foolishly. The only card he had left to play was guilt. If he could dream up something to do while they were gone and make it look like they had left him in the lurch, he could use it to his advantage any time fishing was mentioned in the future. One of the most effective means of motivation in rural Texas in that day was shame. You just cannot beat it when it comes to manipulating anyone who has any sort of conscience. Pa always kept this trump card up his sleeve, and it was this kind of thinking that motivated him on this occasion to try to continue with the harvest before it was dry enough to be feasible.

As Dad told it, he and Bruce were on their way back from a couple of days of livin'. They were within a few miles of the farm when one of them noticed a mysterious piece of machinery sitting idle in I.W.'s field.

"What could that be?" wondered Bruce.

"I don't know," responded Dad. "It's not tall enough to be the combine."

"But it sure is shaped like a combine," noted Bruce.

"Oh no," said Dad, "You don't think I.W. tried to cut wheat while we were gone, do you?"

"I would not put it past him," growled Bruce, "He'd try it, if for no other reason than to spite us!"

As they got closer, they saw that the machine was indeed Pa's combine. It appeared shorter since it was buried up to the feeder-house in mud. Naturally, this sight served as icing on the cake for the fishermen since Pa would surely be sporting a good bit of egg on his face for what was clearly a bungled attempt to induce shame in the duo. Their joy was short-lived, however. When they pulled into the driveway, Pa was there to explain to them, in no uncertain terms, how the whole incident was really their fault.

"I broke two $55 variable speed belts trying to get that combine out while you boys were off fishin'!" Pa spun. The ability to put a dollar figure on the damage made it even more concrete for Pa. As was their custom, they took their medicine with nary a peep, at least until Pa's back was turned.

Another possible means of getting a little time in the mountains was to incorporate something into the trip that made it seem like a legitimate part of the farming enterprise. On one such occasion, Bruce and Dad came up with the idea of taking a wheat truck west on the pretense of gathering lumber for their feedlot enterprise, and sneaking in a little fishing on the sly. Of course, Pa was on to them from the beginning, and he laid out the itinerary. He made it clear that he expected their return within a couple of days, which did not leave them much time to fish.

They tried to overcome the plot with youthful energy, driving down early one morning and loading their lumber by afternoon. Unfortunately, they overestimated their abilities and when they finished loading the wood, headed out on a six mile hike to one of the many promising alpine lakes that dotted the region. They arrived just after dark, having learned a valuable lesson in cartography. Those little squiggly lines running parallel to one another on a topographical map are not artistic shading and the climb was steep. After making a couple of half-hearted casts for good measure, they had to turn around and head right back down, arriving in the wee hours to catch a few minutes of sleep atop their lumber load before heading home. Score one for Pa.

The most ambitious plan they ever hatched involved turning Pa into a fisherman. Many outdoor enthusiasts have fantasized about the possibility of getting their boss hooked on their particular passion, and thus gaining the most powerful of advocates for their cause. Typically, this backfires. If the employer does happen to take to the sport, he is much more likely to leave the original conspirators home to man the fort while he leaves at every whim. This is not what happened with Pa.

He was determined from the beginning to use this opportunity to prove just how wasteful and frivolous this type of trip was. He agreed, begrudgingly, to go along, though he must have been suspicious to get the invitation. By departure time, he was sporting a very sour mood, and it was clear that he intended to make the trip miserable for everyone. Les Barkley, who had married I.W.'s younger daughter, Sharon, was also along on this trip. The Brotherhood of Dean was always very evangelistic, and Uncle Les had been one of the early converts as he had been along on a few Ayres' vacations himself back in the '50s.

There were no super cabs in those days, thus the bench seat of Pa's blue '56 Chevy truck was quite crowded—Les is 6' 4"—so someone had to ride in the camper over the bed. Les was the first victim, but he complained nonstop about how uncomfortable his lanky, stiff frame was in that position. Within a few hours, Dad and Bruce had all of Pa they could stomach anyway, so Pa and Les switched places. They were headed for Charette Lake, and Bruce was driving when they spotted an antelope. Apparently, the excitement of the trip and the sight of wildlife got the best of Bruce. He decided to go off-road in pursuit, to what end, no one is sure. He staunchly claims, to this day, that he forgot that Pa was in the back, snoozing contentedly when they exited the road and bounced out across the pasture.

The camper shell had been built the previous winter by Pa and Dad. It was constructed with masonite, and wound up being quite heavy. Pa's pickup had a somewhat narrow wheelbase anyway, and with its top-heavy shell, the rig was prone to pitch and yaw even when driving on level pavement. Of course, this phenomenon became dangerously pronounced once the truck left the road. To make matters worse, they soon learned that lone antelope do not evade pursuers in a straight line, but tend to weave, which was the last thing this pickup was capable of doing safely. After a chase of unknown duration, during which there were moments when most, if not all of the weight of the vehicle was being carried by only two of the four wheels, it became clear that the creature's home field advantage was insurmountable, and Bruce conceded victory to the antelope.

Only after they came to a stop did they hear the moans emanating from beneath the camper shell. The camping equipment, including a cast iron frying pan, a large metal cooler, and a couple of hefty tackle boxes, had resituated from what had been a tidy arrangement before the chase. Meanwhile, Pa had shifted from his relatively comfortable position atop the gear to one down near the bottom. After a brief excavation of gear, the three found Pa, who was mumbling incoherently, "How many times did we go around that lake... weaving this way and that....with all those pots and pans!" They didn't have the heart to tell him they'd been chasing antelope and weren't even close to the lake yet. As you can imagine, they were unable to make a fisherman out of Pa after that.

Once at the lake, Les failed to heed the warnings about the ferocity of Charette trout and kicked over his tackle box when he got his first thunderous strike. Finding humor in the misfortune of others is a common characteristic of the Brotherhood, and Dad relished each chance he got to describe the sound of every one of Les' brand new spinners tinkling down through the rocks into oblivion. Les voluntarily became what one might call an honorary member of the Brotherhood right about this time. However, that might have something to do with that fact that his first child, a.k.a. "Cousin Barry", was born later that summer. Activity in the Brotherhood always seemed to take a nosedive when one of us kids came on the scene.

Fueled largely with information from Allen Byers, keeping their ears pealed and their pockets stuffed with brochures, the Brotherhood eventually scouted out an extensive list of fishing sites. If you were to put pins in a map you would have a veritable corridor of livin' that cut across the Sangre de Cristos of north central New Mexico and on into the San Juan Mountains of south-central Colorado. Between 1962 and 1965, there are pictures recording various trips along this corridor: from Charette Lakes on to the Cimarron River, past Eagle's Nest Lake, through Red River and on to Questa and the Rio Grande. More pictures exist to show that trips continued through to Chama and into Colorado where they rumbled up the washboard road all the way to Platoro Reservoir. From the number of pictures taken and the variety of locations, I can only conclude that the youthful energy of the Brotherhood won out over Pa's seasoned stubbornness.

Reel Livin'

In the summer of 1964, a decade or so after Dad's first foray into the Rockies, a trip to the Rio Grande was made in Bruce's Volkswagen. It was a tight fit for Dean, Rosie, Bruce, and his bride, Martha. Somehow, they made room for a six-month-old infant(though I don't remember much of the trip), and the Brotherhood of Dean inaugurated its second generation. Actually, I had already been to the Conejos *in utero* during the previous summer, but there is no clear consensus when livin' begins. I was quite a butterball, but they lugged me down into the gorge and back out again, nonetheless. The fishing was cut short when I grew hungry; Rosie and Dean realized that they had left my formula back on the rim. That same summer, my parents put my mattress in the back seat of their coral-colored Ford and headed to Yellowstone. I guess you could say I was livin' before I even knew what it meant to be alive.

Pictures of the Brotherhood from that era end abruptly that summer. More accurately, pictures of fish and smiling fishermen gave way to photos of infants and toddlers. In a way, I feel a bit guilty that I intruded on such a sacred pursuit. Then again, the choice was not mine to make. Besides, the infants and toddlers soon appeared in the pictures with fishing rods in their hands. The cycle of nature distills the silted water of the panhandle and drops it, crystal clear once again, upon the lofty peaks. So too time, with tremendous patience from the charter members of the Brotherhood, finds boys turning to men. They stand beside their heroes as fishing buddies, joining the sacred pursuit and the priceless fellowship of the Brotherhood of Dean—the Brotherhood of 'Livin'.

Chapter 6

Pre-Traumatic Incident Disorder

Dad was not exactly "green" in terms of conservation, and he intimated that such "political correctness" was just a cloak for snobbery. Riparian habitat was sacred only in that it was the holiest of all places to experience "livin'," i.e., the best place to set up camp. Guidelines and restrictions about where and where not to camp existed primarily to keep the off-limit sites pristine so we could camp there.

"They just make those rules for people who don't know what they're doing," Dad might explain if challenged. I rarely challenged him, of course, because it felt wrong, and because I had never seen the approach succeed with him. He treated the great outdoors with an instinctive respect, and quite a bit better than he treated the great indoors, or himself, for that matter. I do remember commenting once on the strands of leftover spaghetti I noticed waving in the waters of the Costilla River:

"Noodlin' for trout, Dean?"

"No," he responded sheepishly. "I thought that would wash away." It did not. Somehow, it managed to get a foothold on the slick rocks right out in the middle of the stream, its blond color standing out in bold contrast to the dark green river bed. Ironically, slick spaghetti and slick rocks manage to hang on to each other quite tenaciously. It makes me wonder if I am taking the wrong approach to secure wading. Maybe I should replace my felt soles with something flour based—like pasta.

When possible, Dad preferred to get his rig as close to the bank of the lake or stream as he could, leaving only enough grass between us and the water to make a nice front lawn for the duration of our stay. There are few places remote enough to get away with this anymore, even with a tent, much less with a 1968 Starcraft pop-up with only six inches of clearance.

When we were planning a trip, just the thought of being anywhere but where we lived was satisfying. However, once we got there, wherever "there" happened to be, we always became significantly more choosey. Once we were in the mountains, one would think that the heavenly setting would suffice, but we found it difficult to settle and usually spent a good bit of time seeking out the perfect repose within that heavenly setting.

The exact placement of the camper in its determined position is one of the most critical decisions we campers make. It
can literally make or break the trip. The pop-up was 8'x14' fully
extended. That meant that we had the mind-boggling task of putting our 108 square feet in the perfect spot, one that would maximize and optimize our "livin'" experience, within, say, a 33,428-
acre state park. When you have trouble deciding between parking
spots at Wal-Mart this can be a daunting prospect.

Fortunately, we considered this process a part of "livin'",
so we did not see it as wasted time. Anyone who complained
was reminded that he could be in the cab of a tractor, or painting
a house in Gruver where it was 98 degrees in the shade and the
wind was blowing 30 miles per hour. Those kinds of reminders
put the kibosh on complaints.

Once the spot had been debated, deliberated, and chosen—a process that could take several hours—the angle of the
camper and the direction in which the door opened had to be carefully considered in order to maximize the emotional impact of the
view as we stepped out the door or looked out the window. When
you only feel alive five days out of the year, you don't want to
leave anything to chance. Even six or seven inches one way or
another can be critical.

"We want to see that patch of aspens, in their full fall glory, over on that hill. And it would be nice if we could watch the
sun set between those two peaks every evening. We need to be
close enough to the river to hear the fish if they start feeding. It
looks like there might be a family of squirrels that would be fun
to watch in that Douglas fir, and we need to be able to see that
deer trail across the meadow…"

Most importantly, we wanted to be invisible from the
nearest road. Invisibility was a critical concern for Dad all the

time, even when he was in a crowd, but especially when he was "livin'". The appearance of another person, especially the wrong kind of person, could jeopardize the entire affair. He certainly did not want to run into someone he did not know, since that induced high trauma. On the other hand, he only liked roughly one out of every 100 people he did know, and he did not want to run into any of them either! Then again, for all his antisocial posturing, often I'd return from an afternoon on the river to discover that Dad had struck up a friendship with someone. Against all odds, that person usually turned out to be a "pretty good ol' boy."

Little was known of conditions like post-traumatic stress disorder in Dad's day. Today, doctors would likely diagnose him with something like pre-traumatic incident disorder (PTID); that is, he lived with recurring visions of scarring encounters and troubling events that might lie in the future, rather than the past. After all, the pre-enjoyment of an experience by "looking forward" to it must be counterbalanced with an equal amount of worry and anxiety about what might go wrong. Without the latter, one is in danger of winding up with a net surplus of joy. This leads to happiness, which is very difficult to suppress. Of course, the expression of happiness should be rare and short-lived, since it is the hallmark of silliness and the primary characteristic of the fool. When we were young, Dad was always careful to monitor our facial expressions in public, lest one of us get caught by the world at large sporting what he called a "shit eating grin."

Naturally, pre-traumatic incident disorder is a critical factor in maintaining a constant pain in the ass quotient. If things are going too smoothly and the PIAQ is in jeopardy, equilibrium can be restored by incorporating a bit of PTID. No doubt, Dad had honed this skill as he sat in on conversations with local farmers who are masters of pessimism.

"Sure has been a wet fall," (which is generally considered a good thing)

"Yep, you know what that means; we are in for a rough winter!"

Pre-traumatic incident disorder is not difficult to master since it is not subject to the laws of logic. In fact, anxiety and worry are often best exercised independent of reason. As in:

"Boy, this has been a wet spring," (again, a good thing),

"Yes sir, 'fraid we got all our rain early; gonna be a long dry summer."

Next year you may hear the same farmers speculate, "We haven't got a drop of rain this fall."

"Yep, I'd say we're on the front end of a drought cycle."

PTID also serves to grease the mechanisms that lead to temper tantrums. Happy people, silly fools, rarely engage in PTID, so they are at a disadvantage when things go wrong. They have to work through a preparatory stage of frustration before they can move on to authentic fits of rage. PTID enables a person to carry this frustration constantly just below the surface. The pump is always primed, if you will. That's why happy people—look for the "shit eating grin"—usually accuse the practitioner of the PTID of overreacting. In truth, the happy person has simply failed to see what just happened in the context of everything that might have, or may be about to happen—poor sap!

Dad was always extremely conscious of the toll a road or trail might take on his vehicle and trailer. Hence, his pre-traumatic incident disorder was usually flaring by the time we scouted the final few hundred feet to the ideal spot. At this point, we had typically spent an hour or more on some unpaved road that, in Dad's mind, was just itching to leave him bereft of hubcaps and tailpipe. He always knew that potholes and rough spots were part of getting to where he wanted to be and this was a source of much pre-trauma.

He was particularly irritated with washboarding, that rippling effect that sometimes characterizes unpaved back roads. He was always anxious to get "there," and just about the time he reached cruising speed, about 25 mph for him, he would invariably encounter one of these sections. It would begin with slight vibrations and quickly crescendo as the suspension of the old red Ford sprang spastically in a vain attempt to keep up with the uneven nature of the road.

The contents of the dash, which could be anything from open cans of shoestring potatoes to hemorrhoid suppositories, along with several dozen fast food salt packets—you can never have too much salt—would first jiggle, and then drop in rhythmic crescendo off the lower side. Onto the floorboard it would go to join the rest of the flotsam and jetsam that was accumulating. By the time he reached the teeth chattering stage of these sections of road, he would be worked up and letting rip with the overture to the SOB shuffle—without the shuffle. About the time he was able to slow the rig down, the road would smooth out again and the process would repeat itself.

After a few minutes of this, Dad convinced himself that this condition was part of a conspiracy. The logic went something like this: The fellows who had to maintain these roads, right here in the middle of paradise, were sour and jaded by years of being in such a beautiful setting, and never getting to enjoy the benefits. They felt like Dad did when he was driving a tractor, only they could see what they were missing. For this reason they came, in time, to resent anyone who was there for purposes of enjoyment. When Dad explained it, we could almost imagine the sinister sneers on their faces as they manipulated their grader blades in an attempt to make the trip as miserable as possible for vacationers. They probably had video cameras hidden in the trees beside these sections, so they could see first hand the havoc they wreaked!

When it comes to camping, the more difficult a spot is to access, the more ideal it tends to be and vice versa. The first challenge was getting off the main road and on to whatever trail led to the prime spot. At this point, all the occupants would disembark to study and discuss the angle of the descent and the height of the initial drop off. If it seemed doable, which depended primarily on Dad's disposition at the moment, we would then begin to take note of any large rocks or downed timber that we might be able to move out of the way, along with any deep holes or immovable objects that might be waiting to snag our undercarriage. The pop-up camper had built-in leveling jacks mounted on each corner so that the gross clearance of six inches really amounted to a net of about three and one half inches.

High up in the Valle Vidal in northeastern New Mexico one summer, we were at just such a stage in our adventure, and had put several miles of washboard road behind us. Little was left on the dashboard. After careful examination, and the removal of what could be moved, Brian and I were each assigned our positions as land guides. We would have to signal, with the prescribed gestures, any course change that Dad might need to make as he eased off the main road.

Scrapes in the finish of his F-150 were particularly irritating for Dad. This was hard for us to understand, since, as his work truck, it regularly received unintentional touch-ups with DuPont latex house paint, usually white, when it happened to be parked downwind of his paint sprayer during a job. Originally a dark cherry red, by this time the truck was as speckled as an exotic bird egg. Nevertheless, we were both assigned a specific tree branch on our respective side of the road, which we were to hold back out of the way so that he would have more room to maneuver.

Dad tentatively backed the camper down the main road so that he could approach at the agreed upon angle, and with everything lined up. Since the pop-up was no wider than the pickup, it was difficult to keep things straight when travelling backwards, even for an old pro like Dad. He jackknifed the rig a couple of times on his way back, and we could see by his expression, and the muffled commentary leaking out of the cab, that his PTID was approaching red line, the point at which all reason and prudence would be abandoned, and just about anything could happen. There would definitely be property damage and possibly serious personal injury, mostly self-inflicted.

By the time he got the camper lined up like he wanted, he was almost 100 yards back down the road, and starting smack dab in the middle of a gnarly washboard patch.

"He's sure a long ways back," noted Brian. "I hope he doesn't get up too much speed."

At this point, Dean's mind was apparently divided as to the ideal speed of approach. On the one hand, the slower he went, the less damage he would incur if something went wrong. On the other, the faster he went, the less likely he would be to get hung up if something dragged. He certainly did not want to be stuck halfway off the road out here in the middle of nowhere. These two opposing possibilities were tugging at one another as he began his approach. Apparently, he decided to use the safer slower speed for the first 50 yards, and then increase to the drag-free, jump speed for the last 50.

"Boy!" I said. "He's getting up quite a head of steam!"

"He sure is," responded Brian. "I don't think this is going to work."

In these situations, I had learned to follow Dad's instructions regardless of the perceived outcome, so that, if anything went wrong, I could not be accused of altering the plan. Brian had less experience and was able to convince himself that his "better ideas" would be warmly received and implemented. He let go of his branch and tried to wave Dad off, so we could reassess the plan. It soon became clear, from the flying gravel and the glazed over look in Dad's eyes, that he was past the point of no return.

"Is he even looking at us?" Brian screamed as he waved frantically.

Dad was still accelerating and already going five mph faster than he had since we left the pavement three hours ago. We could see him clearly now, his teeth clenched tightly around his unlit Swisher Sweet with both hands on the wheel. That meant he had stowed his jumbo Diet Coke, which is the signal that there would be no turning back. He did not see Brian's waving, but he did notice the tree branch Brian had been holding back as it swung out into his path. His eyes, which had closed into narrow slits of concentration, like the Outlaw Josey Wales just before a duel, suddenly popped wide open. As his front tires left the dirt road, I could read his lips as they formed the phrase, "What the hell???" around his cigar. The sight of Brian's branch caused Dad to veer my way instinctively. At that point, I dove for cover, releasing my branch as he flew by in a hail of profanity and a cloud of gravel and dust. It took him a couple of dozen feet to bring the rig to a stop, and we were not in any hurry to cover the distance.

"Why the hell did you let go of those branches?" he cried as he exited the cloud of dust, which was already beginning to stick to his right side, where most of his Diet Coke had landed.

Brian, true to form, tried to plead his case. "You were going too fast! I was trying to get you to slow down!" I stood still and made like a hole in the wilderness so as not to distract Dad from focusing on Brian as the culprit.

"By slamming a pine branch into my windshield?" Dad spat.

"How was I supposed to stop you?" asked Brian.

"Stop me?" Dad replied. "That was not your job! You were supposed to hold back that damn tree branch!"

Meanwhile I started gathering up pieces of camper—a couple of the jacks, some trim, one of the brake light covers, and several Styrofoam cups that had escaped the bed of the truck. We made a formal assessment of the damage, which turned out to be far less than Dad's reaction might have indicated. He predicted that the gas tank and the oil pan would be punctured, which meant that we were stranded and would have to ask for help or batten down the hatches and try to ride out the winter. Faced with these two choices, Brian and I knew that if it were up to Dad, which it probably would be, we would need to start scavenging for berries and roots right away.

Not only did the damage turn out to be minor, but the gross clearance, after this incident, was equal to the net clearance after we removed the two surviving jacks. Now we could get into even tougher spots! Inspired by this possibility, Dad turned his attention back to the next leg of the adventure.

"Now boys," he began. "This next corner is going to be too sharp for me to turn. I'm going to have to pull up between that boulder and that tree, and then back it down to the next switch-back. You two stand on either side of the road and make sure I don't hit anything. And watch those damn tree branches!"

We scratched our heads and looked at each other as he climbed back into the cab. "When you give directions to someone who is looking in the mirror, do you have to point in the opposite direction of what you really want them to do?" Brian asked. His confidence had flown off with the jacks.

"Not as long as the driver remembers that he has to turn the wheel in the opposite direction of where he wants the trailer to go," I answered.

"So do I point in the direction I want the camper to go, or in the direction I want him to turn the wheel?" Brian wondered. "We are in big trouble aren't we?"

"You have no idea!" I chuckled.

Chapter 7

Sin and the Art of Trolling

"Anything done purely for fun is, by definition, sin." This seems to be the consensus of most folks who are old enough to have survived the Great Depression. This fact becomes clear when discussions about fishing cross certain generational lines. When my wife's father, a very pragmatic, hard-working rancher of rather stoic German heritage, hears that I have been fishing, he always has three questions, "How many did you catch? Were any of them big? Where are they now?"

My answer is always the same. "I did not count. It depends. I threw them back."

Though we have had this conversation dozens of times over the past 25 years, my response is always met with startled incredulity. We have never discussed the answer to the first two questions, as they are completely overshadowed and rendered moot by the third.

"You threw them back?" Leroy asks in astonishment, as if he has never heard this before. "You did not keep any of them?"

"No," I sigh.

The implied question at the root of his confusion is, "Why on earth would a fella go to the trouble of going fishing and not bring back anything to show for his time and effort?" What he actually says is, "You don't like fish?"

"Yes," I reply. "I am very fond of them. That's why I throw them back." This is a vain attempt to sidetrack the conversation with sarcasm, which, I have learned, is a foreign concept among stoic Germans.

"No, I mean to eat?" he clarifies.

"Oh, I love fish," I say. "It's one of my favorite foods." Now he has me right where he wants me.

"Then why didn't you keep any?" he continues. Again the implied logic—stoic Germans are long on logic—is, "Redemption for such recreational selfishness is possible only if the culprit returns with something tangible to justify his flagrant squandering of time and energy; preferably something that he can feed his family, who probably came to the brink of starvation while he was out playing."

When faced with this type of interrogation, the fly-fisherman has in his vest one of two classic responses. If we want to be politically correct, we go "green." We launch into a lecture on biodiversity and population stabilization in today's fragile ecosystem. We use this as justification for what we call "catch and release." I don't recommend this approach with stoic Germans. An honest fisherman just admits that, for most of us, keeping fish usually turns out to be more trouble than it's worth. My experience is that Red Lobster does a better job of cooking fish than I do, and they clean them for me.

This explanation does not wash with Leroy. To a true German, nothing is more trouble than it's worth. In fact, the worth of any activity is directly proportional to its trouble. More often than not, trouble alone is reason enough, in and of itself, to do something. Trouble is good for you. It builds the kind character and stamina you will need for the bigger troubles that lie ahead. I learned this from working with Leroy. Looking for an easier way to do something is a waste of time and a hallmark of laziness. Furthermore, only a fool stops working to ask himself why he is doing this the hard way. Trouble is our lot. It's the curse of the fall. "By the sweat of your brow will you eat bread," says the Good Book. Consequently, sweating at something we do not enjoy is the surest sign that we are in God's will.

My dad was also raised in this paradigm. He stood squarely with one foot in the generation that justifies fishing only as a means of sustenance, and the camp that claims enjoyment is the fisherman's true prey. When relating to others my age, Dad had no problem sharing fishing tales into the wee hours any time he got the chance.

This was not the case when he was dealing with people who represented his father's generation. They were never, under any circumstances, to learn that he had taken time off to go fishing. This was due, in large part, to the ongoing conflict that he and Bruce, his brother-in-law, had with my grandfather when the two worked for him in their youth. I.W. never missed an opportunity to remind them that fishing was an utter waste of time. Such time was to be more nobly spent in the fields, or in the barn cataloguing combine parts, taking inventory of the grommets, or recycling used rivets.

This had a two-pronged effect. First, it made fishing even more alluring to Dad and Bruce, ensuring that they would become hopelessly addicted to the sport. Second, it planted a seed of shame that bore the fruit of self-loathing any time Dad was fishing, or enjoying himself at anything for that matter.

I vividly remember how this shame manifested itself at the end of one of our annual fishing trips. As we neared home, I could tell Dad was becoming increasingly agitated, which was not a foreign state of being for him. I happened to be driving as we entered town, pop-up in tow, and was receiving my final approach instructions. "Don't turn down our street," he said nervously. "I don't want Boots to know what we have been doing." Boots lived across the street from Mom and Dad, and was a "retired" farmer about Pa's age. Boots was a nickname, but we never had occasion nor cause to ascertain his given name. I chuckled, thinking surely Dad was joking.

After all, in a town of 2,000 inhabitants, most of the population knew what we had been up to before we did. However, as we neared Chase Street and I began to brake, Dad bolted upright, "NO! NO! NO!" He yelled. "Go around back, down the alley and park behind the fence. I DON'T WANT BOOTS TO KNOW I HAVE BEEN FISHING!" The conviction behind these words startled me and belied a depth of guilt I had never realized he carried. I learned later that Dad, in his paranoia, had come to believe that some kind of zoning conspiracy in Gruver saw to it that there was at least one representative from Pa's generation planted on each street to keep an eye out for slackers.

Apparently, this shame was deeply rooted and unavoidable. But it could be alleviated, at least to a degree, by catching and keeping as many fish as possible. This gave the enterprise a semblance of practicality that helped justify the selfishness that most farmers—and stoic Germans for that matter—associate with fishing. This is the only way I can explain the obsession Dad had with trolling for trout.

In terms of sport, trolling is only one notch above snagging fish with a bare treble hook. The most effective approach for trolling for trout involves the use of what we called a "Christmas Tree," also known among fishermen as a "cowbell." This contraption consists of light gauge, braided wire adorned with several large, gaudy, inline spinners (copper, silver, and the irresistible holographic), with an assortment of colorful beads between them to break up the monotony. To the terminal end of this rig is tied a few inches of monofilament with a baited hook or lure. They come in varying lengths of three to five feet because, well, sometimes you just "need more cowbell."

The flashing and vibration apparently attract every curious, or perhaps disturbed, fish within a quarter of a mile. For some reason, the same trout that would run for cover in a mountain stream, upon catching a glimpse of the sun reflecting off of your line clippers from 200 yards away, will watch a boat purr by overhead followed by slow moving cowbells that must look like a hallucination from a bad acid trip. The trout then decides that there is nothing suspicious about an earthworm swimming four mph at the tail end of it all. Apparently, the highly evolved survival instincts that make trout so difficult to catch in most situations have not prepared the creature for such a ridiculously blatant approach.

In short, trolling is one of the most effective ways to harvest fish and requires only minimal fishing skills. The only redeeming aspect of taking fish this way is that, at the end of the day, you have a lot of dead fish to show for your time and effort (pictures are mandatory). In Dad's mind, this helped satisfy the demands of people who were too practical to fish for fun and must therefore think less of him for doing so. In fact, you might say we were trolling more for Boots than for trout. But troll we must! So, once a year we dolled out the money for a 14-foot aluminum boat with a two horsepower motor and weighed anchor.

Our base of operations was usually Red River, New Mexico. From there it is only a 30-minute drive to Eagle Nest Lake. If you have to troll, and you want to do it in a mountain setting, Eagle Nest is a great choice. There are some nice rainbows in there, and even some Kokanee salmon. Besides, the people around the lake are not nearly as snooty as some trout fishermen, so no one looks down their nose at you for "harvesting" a few trout. That might have something to do with the fact that this pastime brings quite a bit of money into the community.

The participants of these trolling treks were usually my dad, Brian, our younger brother Ben and me. Four grown men in a 14-foot boat does not leave much elbowroom. The crowding problem was compounded by Dad's proclivity toward what dieticians ignorantly label "junk food." First, a cumbersome metal ice chest of antique vintage, adorned with the Coca-Cola logo in cursive, and filled with enough Coke to float a boat much larger than we could afford, was hoisted aboard. This chest also contained a half-moon of mild longhorn cheddar cheese, a package of bologna (with the red plastic rind), and two six-packs of Hershey bars (one with almonds and one without).

Brown paper grocery sacks housed the rest of the food-stuffs without which any self-respecting fisherman dare not be caught. This included a box of saltine crackers, six cans of Vienna sausages, pork rinds (some plain, some hot-and-spicy), a bag of Ruffles potato chips (sour cream and onion if Dad was in the mood to live large), a box of Ritz crackers, and a tin of sardines in mustard sauce. The last item was included strictly as a deterrent to mutiny.

If you wanted to challenge Dad, you first had to prove your manhood by sharing sardines with him. He took particular delight in the retching that ensued on those rare occasions when one of us decided to step up to the plate. In the event that someone wanted a "home cooked" meal, a loaf of white bread and a jar of Miracle Whip rounded out the fare in what had become, for all practical purposes, a floating galley.

I should mention that this was long before the advent of waterless hand sanitizer, so snacking on the "SS Livin'!" was not for the prissy. The presence of salmon egg juice or power bait was taken care of by a quick wringing of the hands in the lake water. This did not produce anything near clean hands, but it did have a chumming effect. You must understand that our family had an old-school approach to building immunity: 1) Throw as many germs at the child as possible, the earlier in life the better; 2) Take every opportunity to place the child in any environment that is traditionally believed to cause illness. Therefore, there was no big emphasis on hand washing, and we were encouraged to play in the rain and snow as often as possible, preferably with wet hair. Mom staunchly believed that, when treated this way, the body toughened up and became immune to almost anything nature can throw at it. Some might scoff, but the McClenagan boys rarely got sick.

After the food was loaded, there was just enough room for the only other thing that mattered—the fishing gear. Since trolling is largely a matter of chance, the understood rule of thumb was that the number of lines in the water at any given time should never fall below "N+1" where N is equal to the number of people aboard. That required that the number of poles available be no less than twice that number. This allowed for re-rigging in the fashion of musketeers reloading during battle; one person could be preparing the next rig while one line was being brought in so that there was no gap in the offering. Keeping that many rods outfitted demanded our full arsenal of tackle, which meant that everything in the 42-cubic-foot fishing closet in the garage at home had to be divided out between the two rather hefty tackle boxes Dad and I possessed between us.

Almost equal to Dad's shame of fishing for fun was my own shame, as a budding fly-fisherman, in trolling for trout. In order to live with myself, I had to keep at least one fly rod outfitted, though the prospect of making a cast in a boat with three other guys was risky. Besides the obvious danger of incidental body piercing, my rather athletic casting stroke—a tactful way to say "very poor"—was apt to rock the boat, which, when fully loaded, floated mere inches above the water. I was torn between my compulsion to wield the long rod and my lifelong commitment not to "rock the boat" when Dad was around.

The positions aboard the SS Livin' were not so much assigned as understood. Dad manned the stern, since he was the only one he could trust with the complexities of navigation and yeomanship. From there, he tended his pole on one side, Ben's on the other, and the extra clutched deftly between his thighs. From amidships, Brian and I each monitored a pole, one port and one starboard.

Ben occupied the bow, where he fashioned a comfortable looking nest from which he operated a portable radio and perused an assortment of entertainment magazines that he had brought along to pass the time. Dad found this unsettling since he assumed any magazine that did not have a fish or a deer on the cover was more than likely pornographic. With our setup, trolling from the bow was impossible anyway as all the fishing lanes were taken, and this was just fine with Ben. He was along for the company and for the show.

Our day was typically divided into two halves—pre-squall and post-squall. Given the setting and altitude of the lake, we could count on getting caught in at least one downpour rolling out of the mountains to the west, and we invariably managed to be as far from the dock as possible when the storm hit. This dock, the only one on the lake, was located on the west shore so that our attempt to escape took us directly into the teeth of the storm. To make matters worse, the outboards supplied with the rental boats are designed for trolling and don't exactly skip across the lake even when the water is calm, much less when fighting two foot waves and a 25-knot headwind. In fact, the throttle, under those conditions, is little more than ornamental. We had complained about this in the past but were dismissed out of hand. As I recall, the manager tried to skirt the issue with rude questions about gross tonnage and recommended weight limits.

"Bastard just wants to rent us a bigger boat!" Dad explained as we exited.

In the midst of these squalls, the movement of the waves, the passing of the clouds, and the driving rain created the illusion of motion for those of us in the boat. An objective observer from a vantage point onshore, however, would have seen little in the way of forward progress. None of us thought to question why, no matter the severity of the storm, we always arrived back at the dock ten minutes after it was over. We thought it had something to do with Einstein's theory on the relativity of space and time.

Naturally, we were well prepared for such events and carried the necessary equipment to get us through in relative comfort...theoretically. Dad bought at least half a dozen emergency ponchos every year in the months leading up to our vacation. These, of course, we left back at home, which forced us to buy another half-dozen, at twice the cost, once we reached the lake. One emergency poncho comes in a bag about the size of a deck of playing cards. The package contains a picture of an inordinately handsome model enjoying some outdoor activity in the midst of a simulated downpour. This perpetuates two falsehoods: 1) Those of us who hunt and fish are inordinately handsome; 2) You will have time to find and don this glorified trash bag before you get soaked.

Crowded and stocked as the boat was, finding a package that small falls into the needle in a haystack category. In fact, we completely dispensed with that metaphor. In our family, something difficult to find is referred to as "a poncho in a dingy." Our priorities being what they were, food items tended to rise to the top as the day wore on, while everything else sifted toward the depths.

Despite the fact that these showers were routine, they somehow managed to catch us off guard every time. Only when the first big splats hit did we even begin to wonder exactly where in our vessel the ponchos might have drifted. Rainstorms in the mountains tend to be short on the sprinkle stage anyway, so the time between the first drops and total saturation is but a matter of seconds. Those seconds were fraught with tension aboard the SS Livin'.

"Ben!" asked Dad. "Where did you put those ponchos?"

"What ponchos?" asked Ben.

"The emergency ponchos I handed you as we were getting out of the truck!" yelled Dad.

"I don't remember you handing me any ponchos," Ben responds defensively. "You handed me the hibachi."

"The what?" screams Dad, his hearing beginning to fade.

"That little grill," Ben clarifies. "You said Brian likes fried bologna."

"I've never had fried bologna," responds Brian. "But it sounds pretty good!"

"I'm the one that likes fried bologna," I chime in. "It's really good with a dash of lemon pepper on it."

Dad's frustration intensified as the frequency of the splats picked up. "I don't give a damn about any fried bologna!" He yelled. "Who has the ponchos?"

Brian responded in his best Willy Nelson whine,"The day they laid poor Poncho low, Lefty split for O-hi-o…" Brian often broke into song when something reminded him of a tune he knew. The rest of the family had learned early the fine art of tiptoeing around my Dad, especially when he was torqued, but Brian always seemed to rush in, or more likely, stumble in, where angels fear to tread. Dad would usually embark on one of his famous tongue-lashings that withered the rest of us, but Brian would just stare back at him with a blank expression of innocence and say, "Wha'd I do?" Dad would pause for a few seconds, then bust up laughing, along with the rest of us, while Brian kept asking, "No, really. Wha'd I do?"

Brian continued to croon, oblivious to Dad's withering

81

gaze, "Where he got the bread to go…"

"Shut up and find those damn ponchos!" interrupted Dad.

"You know, Dean," Brian began, "All that floating anger you carry is not good for you." Brian was a trained counselor by this point, which meant he just stumbled in from a different direction.

"If you don't want to be a floating jackass," retorted Dad, "you'll start looking for those ponchos!"

Brian turned to me and said, "Wha'd I do?"

The altercation brought Brian's wondering mind back on task. "I think I had the ponchos. They were still in the paper sack. Here they are…oh…wait…. No, that's the Cheese-Whiz. Does anybody know where the Ritz crackers are?"

"To hell with the Ritz crackers," Dad hollered, water dripping from the bill of his cap. "We need those damn ponchos."

"I think you passed that sack to me when we were loading the boat," I reminded Brian. "I stuck them in one of those green creels." We had not used creels to carry fish in years, but we never went anywhere without them and we bought a couple more each year. These were cheap little green bags with vented ends. They had nifty little pockets that were just the right size for a jar of salmon eggs while also sporting a handy 12-inch ruler across the top.

All four of us frantically began checking the creels within reach. We found seven jars of dried up salmon eggs, two Bob Betz worm boxes, quite a bit of grass that we had stuffed in the creels out of habit, a Hershey Bar that had oxidized to a gray-white shade (Brian assured us that it still tasted okay), a tangle of Rapala lures, which Dad found the hard way, and a copy of a 1947 edition of Art Flick's *Streamside Guide to Naturals and*

Their Imitations.

This last find pulled me off task. "Wow, listen to this," I called out, crouching over the volume to protect its yellowing pages from the rain. "'No man is born an artist or an angler, and you cannot make a man that was none, an angler by a book.' Izaak Walton…"

"I don't give a damn what Isaiah Watson has to say unless he knows where those ponchos are!" cried Dad.

"Oh wait!" yelled Brian. "I saw the ponchos in a creel while I was looking for the beef jerky. I thought I had better put them somewhere handy in case we needed to get to them in a hurry." Somewhere handy turned out to be the back pocket of my fly-vest, which I had been wearing all the while.

Finding the emergency poncho is only the first step, and extensive experience has led me to question whether they are intended to remedy emergencies, or cause them. First, the simplicity of their design, four feet of front flap with a matching length of back flap separated by a hooded hole through which one pokes their head, is deceiving. In sunny, calm conditions, this is a snap. It's as easy as tying a complex fishing knot at the kitchen table. Of course, you never tie the knot that really counts, or put on the poncho you really need, at the kitchen table. Something almost sinister happens when wind and water are added to the setting.

One of the main selling points of this garment is its light weight, which makes it easy to store and carry, but very difficult handle when the wind is blowing. Apparently, south of the border, where the poncho first gained popularity, people experience a lot of windless storms. These were not the types of storms we dealt with, however. Four men, each wrestling eight feet of poncho adds up to 32 feet of wet plastic slapping about maliciously in a 14-foot boat.

Naturally, Dad had turned the boat into the storm to put us on a tack that would get us to the dock. Unfortunately, this also put him downwind of most of the whipping plastic. You may have noticed by now that painful and frustrating experiences involving Dad never followed a random pattern. This being the case, you can count on the fact that he was destined to experience more than his fair share of these insulting wallops. To add injury to insult, flapping plastic has an insidious tendency to snag on anything metal. The tail of Brian's poncho seemed particularly malevolent and soon found the pile of lures Dean had recovered from his creel. Most of these were unceremoniously tossed overboard, but a few hung fast and circled about Dad's head like a storm of angry hornets.

The flapping poncho was designed to be brought under control via the use of a series of plastic snaps, male and female, that line the seams down each side of the garment. Finding and correctly aligning these snaps is best achieved by getting into proper rhythm with the slaps one is receiving from the poncho tails. Depending on the type of storm, this may take the 1-2-3, 1-2-3 beat of a waltz (slap, slap, snap, slap slap snap). However, in mountain thundershowers, the cadence is more like a tango; slap, slapetty, slap, snap, slapetty, slap, snap, snap.

Rhythm was never Dad's forte, and the plastic fasteners tend to rip out anyway, so he secured his poncho with a bungee cord about his waist. Bungee cords are, to the outdoor enthusiast, what "gray tape" is to the homemaker, filling a variety of needs, from belts and tourniquets to stringers and tent flap holders.

Once all the poncho tails were brought under subjection, we hunkered down for the ride in. All the fishermen who had been suckered into renting bigger crafts, like pontoon boats with awnings, cruise by us in relative comfort, probably enjoying crackers and fried bologna. As passengers, Brian, Ben and I had the good fortune of being able to turn our backs to the wind and rain. Once again, Dad seemed destined to take the brunt of things since he was the only one who could steer the boat properly. As small pellets of hail shredded the Swisher Sweet cigar he had clenched between his teeth, Ben proposed that he try steering while facing the other way. Unfortunately, it became obvious in short order that where you have been is not a very precise indicator of where you are going. But we were sure we could help.

"She's drifting a bit to port, I think," I yelled.

"What?" screamed Dad.

"Port," I said.

"Port, my ass!" Dad responded. "Just speak English."

"Left," I clarified.

"No!" corrected Brian. "The boat is going left. Turn the motor to the right."

"Wait," I argued. "Don't you turn the motor to the left to turn the boat to the right?"

"Well," Brian countered, "actually, the handle goes to the left, but the motor goes to the right, which makes the boat...I'm getting confused. Hey, these Vienna sausages are pretty good if you dunk them in mustard."

Soon we were sideways and the waves were spilling over into the boat. "You two don't know crap about driving a boat!" Dad said as he turned back around. Brian and I were just a couple of feet from him and face-to-face with his pained expression. The twisting maneuver had shifted his poncho out of alignment and hidden half of his face behind the hood. The Swisher Sweet was soaked and had unraveled so that its remnants were swinging limply from the white filter that was still gripped stubbornly between his teeth.

Unfortunately, we inherited from Dad the ability to find humor in the misfortune of others, and you can't turn that kind of thing off. Out of the corner of my eye, I saw Brian's shoulders beginning to bounce under his poncho. I knew from experience that he was coming at me with that elbow, and once it made contact, there would be a volcanic eruption of tension-induced laughter.

I had no choice but to turn into the rain. I knew which storm I would prefer to face!

I knew I had made the right choice a few seconds later when Brian, unable to shake the Willy Nelson tune from his head, began to sing softly, so that only Ben and I could hear, "The lure my poncho found down South ended up in Daddy's mouth…

Sin and the Art of Trolling

Chapter 8

Row, Row, Row Your Boat

Trolling for trout not only strained my pride as a would-be fly-fisherman, it also limited the geographic range of paradise available to us. Wherever we camped, we had to be within an hour or so of a lake that was big enough for trolling. We made a valiant attempt to circumvent this restriction once, on Lake Isabel in southern Colorado. However, we were put off by the restrictions against motorized crafts. It was difficult to maintain adequate trolling speed by rowing, especially with all that food aboard.

We had heard that trolling on Platoro Reservoir, one of our favorite spots in southern Colorado, could be very productive. However, they don't rent boats there, so you have to drag your own watercraft up 30 miles of washboard roads. We briefly entertained the idea of hitching a boat on behind the pop-up. But it only took a moment's reflection to see that wiring issues alone would put us far beyond the safe operating range of both our Pain in the Ass Quotient(PIAQ) and Dad's Pre-Incident Stress Disorder(PISD).

Another member of the Brotherhood generously offered us the use of his paddleboat, but our cooler alone put us over the weight limit. Besides, we weren't sure any of us had the thigh power to pull four or five cowbells through the water for any length of time, though it might make an excellent event as part of some "World's Strongest Man" competition:

"Heinz has four seconds to make those last 20 feet if he wants to overtake Ulrichckt!" the commentator might say. "He's giving it all he's got, but I'm afraid that three pound rainbow he hooked at the halfway point is going to do him in."

And, so it was, one August day, we found ourselves loitering about the boat shop in Eagle Nest, New Mexico. Dad was arranging for the boat rental and the exchange was taking a little longer than usual as the manager seemed to be trying to explain something to Dad. We could not hear what was being said, but we could interpret Dad's side of the conversation through his body language. Periodically, he was clenching his teeth and sticking out his chin. This meant that he was saying "Yeh," but not understanding a word she said.

Dad was hard of hearing and the problem was compounded by his PISD, especially in social situations in which he was less than comfortable. Essentially, that was any social situation where he was forced to communicate with anyone outside the family or even with more than two family members at one time. During these encounters, the conversation might go as such:

At the grocery store:
Clerk: "Would you like paper or plastic?"
Dad: "Yeh."
Or at a restaurant:
Waitress: "Would like soup or salad with that?"
Dad: "Yeh."
Or at the doctor's office:
Doctor: "Is the pain on your right or left side?"
Dad: "Yeh."

"Try to tell me how to run a boat!" Dad muttered as we left the shop. This he found insulting on two counts. First, real men don't need instructions on how to operate an outboard motor. Second, they certainly do not need such advice from a woman!

The sun had not yet crested the Sangre de Cristos as we puttered away from the dock out into the morning fog. There was not a breath of wind and the surface of the lake was the color of emerald silk. We tried to start a little earlier with every successive venture because Dad always seemed to think we were getting on the water just a few minutes after the fish quit feeding. At the other end of the day, just as we dragged back into the cabin, he would state quite confidently, "We should just be getting out on the lake about now."

Dad was all business and in the zone, but he took a moment to remind us, "Now boys, this is livin'." He sported a look of intense concentration—or perhaps constipation, one never knew—his unlit Swisher Sweet at attention between his tightly drawn lips. Those of us who were fishing eagerly awaited his cue to start letting out line when the time was right. Until we determined what the fish were biting on any given day, we kept a variety of baits in the water to cover our bases—at least one night crawler, some salmon eggs, a couple of flavors of power bait, and a Panther Martin spinner. Dad kept track of what everyone was using at any given moment so that he could fill in any gaps in our offering.

As usual, Brian was borrowing from my arsenal of equipment, though he had shelled out $7 for a four foot cowbell rig. His was the first incident of the day. Apparently, the last time I had put new line on my old Millionaire bait-casting reel, which I never learned to cast and used only for trolling, I had been a bit careless tying the arbor knot that secured the line to the spool of the reel. It should not have been an issue since the reel held over 300 yards of eight pound test line, far more than could safely be let out trolling.

Brian, however, was of the opinion that the fellow with the most line out was fishing uncharted waters and had the best chance of hooking into one of the lake's fabled five pound rainbows whose ancestors' pictures adorned the walls of the bait shop. He was chatting away, as is his manner, and I was only able to draw his attention back to his pole in time for him to watch the tale end of his line snake smoothly through the guides of the rod. It settled momentarily on the surface film of the lake before sinking into the mossy green depths.

Dad had an uncanny knack for sensing and exploiting frustration in others as a form of personal entertainment. He could smell it like a shark smells blood in the water, and he began circling and brushing up against Brian to see if he was worth a nibble.

"Hey, Brian," he asked with mock curiosity, "You didn't buy one of those long Christmas Trees, you know, the $7 ones, did you?"

"Hell Yes!" said Brian. "It was over $8 with tax!"

"Well Brian, what did you do that for?" continued Dad, his tone dripping with condescension.

"It's not like I planned to lose the damn thing!" responded Brian, his face reddening by the second. "Besides, if 'Mr. Field and Stream' here could tie all these fancy knots he can name, this never would have happened." He added, waving toward me.

"It would not have mattered if you had been watching what you were doing," I countered. "As much line as you had out, your cowbell is probably still back on the dock anyway."

Ben grinned over the top of the most recent issue of the *National Enquirer* from his nest in the bow of boat. "Do you want a magazine, Brian?" He quipped. "I think it would be a lot more relaxing than what you guys are doing."

Dean brought the boat around so we could try to snag Brian's line, but in the half mile it took us to come about—you cannot turn a very tight circle with four lines out—we lost our bearings. We made a couple of passes where we thought the line might be, and finally chalked it up as a loss. Getting tangled with another line is one of those things you can hardly avoid when you don't want it to happen, but can never seem to achieve when you do.

Brian muttered about his financial misfortune while I set up another reel for him. Meanwhile, Dad kept a sharp eye out for any signs of action from other boats on the lake. Trolling is a hit and miss venture, and it's human nature to assume that you would be catching more fish if you were "over there" instead of "here." As a result, trollers tend to wind up chasing each other around the lake thinking that the other guy might be on to something. Of course, the other guy is following another boat that is following the boat that is following you. As more and more boats get on the water, it turns into a kind of complex square dance.

By the time I had Brian's rig ready, he had seen an eagle in the distance and was heartily crescendoing into the introduction of The Eagle and the Hawk, a John Denver tune, as he let out his line.

"ooooOOOOHHHHHHHH, I am the eagle, I live in high country..." he began. "In rocky cathedrals that ...Whoa! Hey, kill it! Kill it! Kill it!" This cry served as the signal to the helmsman to shut down the motor and thereby decrease the resistance while the fortunate fisherman brought home his prize. All that cowbell metal spinning in the water creates a good bit of drag, such that one's pole sports a pronounced bend even when there is no fish on it. As a result, fish under 12 inches are sometimes hard to detect, and it's not unusual to drag one to death—drown it, ironically—without ever realizing you have a bite. Standard operating procedure demands shutting down the engine any time someone thinks they might have a fish.

"I don't think I got him," said Brian as the boat slowed and the tension on his rod eased. "Wait! There he is!" He corrected. "Oh man! This feels like a good one!" I did not doubt this, since Brian had this annoying habit of out-fishing those of us who were hopelessly addicted to the sport on those rare occasions when he decided it was worth the trouble to come along.

"Get your rod tip up!" coached Dad.

"What?" snapped Brian, already feeling the pressure of this close supervision.

"Don't let him take you down into the moss," continued Dad. "You're givin' him too much slack! You're gonna lose him!"

As Brian raised the rod, the fish, still 30 yards out, leapt about two feet out of the water, flashing silver in the morning sun that had just emerged from the fog. "Oh #$%&!" cried Brian when he saw the fish. It did appear to be a monster, as good as or better than any we had ever caught here. This fact only served to increase the pressure Brian was already feeling. The instant the trout hit the water, it began a strong run.

"You're horsing him, Brian," instructed Dad. "He's gonna break off!"

"You said not to give him any slack," replied Brian. "I'm trying to keep him out of the damn moss!"

"Well, you can't horse him," responded Dean, who was clearly beginning to enjoy Brian's frustration.

I thought I might as well get in on the fun, "How do you have the drag set on that reel?" I asked.

"Drag!" Brian screamed. "It's your reel. I thought you set the drag."

"No," I replied. "Let me think. If I remember right, the last time I used that reel I was fishing for bass with 14-pound test, so it's probably set pretty tight."

"14-pound test!" Brian said, turning a bit white. "What's on there now?"

"Oh, it's still 14-pound test," I explained.

"Good!" Brian replied.

"But I think I put six feet of four pound tippet on the end," I added just to stoke the coals.

"FOUR!?" screamed Brian. "How the hell am I supposed to land this monster on four pound test?"

"Well, you have to set the drag just so and keep pressure on him, but you can't horse him," I offered. "Weren't you listening on the way over when I read that article on how to play a large fish?" I caught a lot of chiding for always having my head in a magazine, so I made use of every opportunity to return the digs. By this time, the trout was within ten feet of the boat, and there was a lot more pressure on Brian than on the fish.

"Watch it!" hollered Dad. "Don't let him get the line around the prop. Be careful now, you're horsing him again!" Brian was muttering a steady stream of obscenities as the fish got close enough for us to see that it was indeed a rainbow in the 22 to 25 inch range.

Dad was poised with the net, and I was leaning over the rail of the other side of the boat providing counterbalance. Ben had lowered his magazine by this time.

"When he sees the boat," began Dad, "he'll probably make one more..." At that moment, Brian's rod bowed double as the fish dashed under the boat. I grimaced at the resounding "thunk" of the fish slamming into the bottom on the aluminum boat. The line went slack immediately, and the sky turned blue with profanity.

"Did you lose him, Brian?" asked Dad. "You didn't lose that fish did you?"

At this point, given the size of the fish, and how close Brian had come to landing him, I felt any further teasing would be in bad form. Dad, however, was just getting started. "Well Brian," he drawled in a condescending "you should know better" tone. This opening signaled that he was about to launch into one of his classic, merciless barrages. "You know what happened, don't you Brian?" he asked.

"Yeh," yelled Brian, "the mother%$#%^ son of a ^%$%# broke my @#$% four pound tippet!"

"Well, yeh," Dad replied calmly. "That's because you were horsing him."

"Bull&%#%!" responded Brian.

"Boy," continued Dad, "that was a good fish too. How much do you think he weighed?" I was not about to join in the brutality. "At least four pounds, I bet," he added. "I told you not to horse him."

I thought Dad was way over the line at this point. Based on what happened next, I have to think that the Man upstairs felt the same way. Dad, still grinning around his Swisher Sweet, gave a hardy tug on the starter rope of the Johnson outboard. It moved about four inches before stopping dead, jerking the T-handle out of his hand. The grin had faded by the time he made his second attempt. This time, his grip was firmer, but the rope stopped anyway snapping and retracting back into the housing of the motor leaving Dad holding the rubber T. The last echo of Brian's tirade had just died away as Dad's began.

On those rare occasions when Dad allowed himself to do something he enjoyed, he was always anxious, as if he were waiting for the other shoe to drop. He seemed to have the sneaking suspicion that something or someone, somewhere or somehow, was plotting to sabotage the fun at any moment. A $75 rental boat threatening to leave him stranded in the middle of a lake was evidence of just this kind of conspiracy.

Truth be told, Dad had a love-hate relationship with outboard motors, and none of these ventures passed without some kind of altercation between the two. All of us, including Dad, knew this, so the pump was already primed when the moment came, and things turned personal quickly.

To make matters worse, I noticed that Dad was already showing signs of the early stages of "raw ass." This is a debilitating condition that results from some kind of chemical reaction between the aluminum seat of a boat and the cotton underpants of the fisherman. Apparently, these two otherwise stable compounds, in the presence of even a small amount of heat and sweat, combine to form some kind of some kind of corrosive irritant. It begins with a tingling sensation in the buttocks, and quickly progresses to the point where one's underwear, which seemed soft and comfortable just moments before, feels like 60-grit sandpaper. The natural reaction is to scratch, which only serves to invigorate the blood supply to the affected region, and catalyzes the reaction. Before long, it feels as if your underwear is full of sand burs. Passing boaters should remember that their time is coming, and are expected to look away politely if they notice someone dipping his butt cheeks into the cool waters for relief. This is the type of etiquette you will not see in "Hints from Heloise."

When Brian saw the T-handle in Dad's hand, he could not pass up the opportunity for a little payback and commented, "You shouldn't have horsed it, Dean." Fortunately, the spike in blood pressure had already rendered Dad deaf, though clearly not mute. He gave the engine, its manufacturer, and the watercraft industry in general, a colorful tongue-lashing as he removed the cover of the motor. A veteran shade-tree mechanic, Dad was sure there was no such thing as a problem he could not fix, even if it meant performing a floating overhaul with his pocketknife and fishing pliers.

These tools were quickly deemed worthless, and were cast overboard, where they would receive their just desserts for failing him. The pull cord would not budge and he was unable to ascertain the reason for this stubbornness. Bereft of tools, he soon resorted to a series of violent blows on the housing of the motor with his aluminum rod case, accompanied by a running commentary on the sordid ancestry of the rental manager and her staff. Alas, this failed to free the starter rope. Within short order, Dad was entertaining aloud the idea of giving this ^$$%$ %$#$$ #%@^$$ outboard a "burial at sea," as a means of teaching it a lesson. As he ratcheted up his eulogy, I noticed that the motor was fastened to the boat with two simple screw clamps, which would make the plan he had in mind far too simple to perform.

It was clear by then that Dad had turned a corner. The expression of anger is an art form for some, and once they get so far into a masterpiece, they refuse to be distracted by possible solutions. Once Dad reached this point, he eschewed rational solutions, mocked advice, and deftly batted down all attempts to help, choosing, instead, any action that might make the situation worse. It's embarrassing to exhibit anger that is out of proportion with the trouble at hand, so it's in the best interest of the angered to make things worse in an attempt to bring them up to par with the fit *de jour*, or the fit *de heure*, as the case may be.

The three of us knew from experience that we would not be allowed to help overtly. So, using only hand signals, and taking care not to be noticed, Brian and I took up oars. Our plan was to make it appear that fair winds had gently propelled us the half mile back to the dock. In fact, we were drifting along a course that, without intervention, would have us run aground a mile from the dock…if we swam. The walk would have been more like 3 miles.

Unfortunately, we had neither cause nor opportunity to develop much in the way of rowing skills growing up in the panhandle of Texas. It's a lot harder than it looks, especially if you are trying to be sneaky about it. As a result, the boat was mostly spinning in half circles, and making little in the way of forward progress. Ben, from his point of view as a detached observer, was the first to notice the humor in our situation, and he snickered. This sound coupled with the tension in the air, initiated a spasm of "funeral giggles" among the three of us.

A funeral giggle is a universal phenomenon that causes humans to laugh in the most inappropriate of times and circumstances. Dad was facing the other way, completely absorbed in his own personal war. He was looking for matches, having determined that a small fire atop the crankcase might loosen things up. The first attack of laughter was controlled and we were able to cover with mock coughing. But when the boat began to spin off course yet again, we broke down and the vessel rocked with laughter.

This broke Dad's fixed concentration, and he turned to see what was going on. "You two think you are going to get us back to the dock? You guys aren't doing shit!" I know this sounds harsh, but you have to understand Dad's perspective. The oars in our hands were a clear implication that we doubted him. They gave voice to his unspoken belief that we did not think he was going to be able to get the motor running, and he was supremely insulted.

There was a moment of silence as the words sank in. Then, as they bounced back off the mountains in a decrescendo, "SHIT, SHIt, SHit, Shit, shit, shi, sh..." we collapsed in uncontrollable laughter, heedless of the consequences. A grin even slipped out from around Dad's Swisher Sweet before he could turn back to the motor.

We did eventually get to the dock. Brian felt compelled to declare with pride, "I guess we were doing shit, after all!" Fortunately, the threads on the screw clamps that held the outboard were quite rusty, so Dad was unable to execute his *piece de re-sistance*. However, he had another plan hatched by the time we secured the boat.

"Warren," he commanded, "you stay here with the boat while I go up and take care of this." His tone was ominous. "And if they send somebody down here, don't you let them in this damn boat!" Dad did not want anyone to get there and fix the problem before he had a chance to act out his rage in the presence of those who were closest to being responsible.

Brian whispered, "I'd better go with him. Maybe I can calm him down."

"Oh, yeh," I responded, "You've always had a knack for doing that!"

As it turned out, Ben and Brian both accompanied Dad, leaving me to guard the boat. It was just a quarter mile or so to the shop, and they had been there only a minute before a truck pulled out and headed my way. This did not give me much time to form a reason, much less a plan, for keeping the staff out of their boat. Two guys in their late teens jumped out of the truck and trotted down to the water's edge.

"Having trouble?" one of them asked.

"Yeh," I said. "We can't get the motor started—rope's stuck." In my mind, these words were spoken very sternly, with an air of contempt, and tainted with disgust, just as Dad would have said them. In fact, they came out sounding quite civil, which disappointed me. If I had had a Swisher Sweet in my mouth, I'm sure things would have sounded different. Furthermore, I was unable to assume a very menacing pose from my position in the boat, astride the antique Coke cooler. My only hope now was that some code of maritime etiquette would keep them from boarding without an invitation. But apparently, you have to rent a bigger boat to get the benefits of such courtesy. I was outnumbered, and tired from all the rowing, so I did not put up a fight when one of them promptly boarded without ceremony. Truth be told, I am not the type of person you want to ask save seats for you, much less guard someone from their own property. "Let the whipper-snapper have a shot at it!" I reasoned.

From the bow, I could not see exactly what was going on, but in a couple of pulls, the young yeoman had the motor purring again. "Nothing wrong with this," he said, grinning as if this was not the first time this had happened. "You know you have to have the throttle in neutral to start the motor, don't you?"

"Neutral, uh, okay, sure," I stammered.

I got the report about what transpired at the boathouse from Brian. Dad stormed in with the air of one primed to dole out an ass-whuppin', all bluff, of course. But he had to wait in line at the counter. This delay gave him time to compose himself, which was not part of the plan. Once he worked up a good head of steam, the last thing he wanted was time to gain some perspective that was liable to take all the sting out of his delivery. When he finally got to the front of the line, I'm sure some of the more expressive expletives had been weeded out of his scripted address.

"That damn boat you rented us is not worth a crap!" he spouted. His teeth were still clenched, though he had removed the stub of his cigar that had become a prop for the effect he hoped to achieve. He pointed it in the general direction of the boat.

"Can you be a little more specific?" responded the clerk.

"What?" asked Dad. Listening to what she had to say was not a part of the scene as he had envisioned it. Fortunately, the sarcasm did not register with him.

"What's wrong with the boat?" she clarified.

"The damn motor won't start!" he explained. It was at this point that the two troubleshooters headed out the back door.

"Did you have it neutral?" she asked

"My boys had to row that son-of-a-bitch in from two miles out!" Dad exaggerated, staying with the script, and beginning to get his old form back.

"Sir, did you have the throttle in neutral? She asked again, enunciating a little more clearly this time. "These new motors won't start unless you have the throttle in neutral."

"We paid $75..." Dad started before the question sank in. "What?" he asked as he transitioned from rage to embarrassment.

She repeated the information.

Dad clamored for the upper hand, "Neutral! Hell, I don't know if it was in neutral. The rope was stuck. I've been using outboard motors since I was 13 and I've never seen one that had to be in neutral to start!"

"I'm sorry for your inconvenience, sir." she replied, "But I went over this with you when you rented the boat this morning." Nothing is more damaging to a fellow's spirit of ass-whuppin than politeness.

"Well," he said, standing down, "We'd better not have any more trouble with it." The rage was quickly giving way to guilt and embarrassment, as he turned to stomp away. He took one step then turned back and said in a most civil tone, "Oh, could I have another jar of that rainbow power bait, and one of those three foot cowbells. My son here lost his trying to horse in a fish."

I don't think she recognized that this amounted to a gracious apology from Dad.

Chapter 9

You Bear! Shoo!

By the fall of 1999, my dad and I had permanently carved into our schedules yearly fall fly-fishing trips to the mountains of New Mexico and southern Colorado. The rest of life was co-ordinated around this trip, and what could not be made to fit was summarily eliminated. It seems only fitting, in hindsight, that the events of that fall's outing, our last together, gave our ventures the title by which they will forever be remembered: "The Annual, You Bear! Shoo! Fall Fly-Fishing Extravaganza."

My brother, Brian, was along this particular fall. He was not able to get away for every trip, but had managed to make an appearance every third or fourth year for the past seven. This made him the brunt of a great deal of ribbing concerning how soft and citified he was becoming when compared to the sourdoughs we deemed ourselves to be. He still worried about losing favor with his wife, tried to maintain regular bowel movements, washed his hands, and changed underwear daily—the kinds of things Dad and I had long since given up.

Though we had shared countless hours together on the banks of local catfish ponds in our childhood, Brian never got the fishing fever. He became the type of fisherman who loses most of his tackle between outings, and it fell to me to outfit him anew when he was along. Typically, he borrowed a couple of my meticulously hand-tied flies, the names of which he staunchly refused to learn despite my incessant lecturing, and half-hitched them below a bubble cork on his shiny new Wal-Mart rig.

In the time it took me to gear up for what would be a six to eight hour assault on the river—yielding maybe a dozen fish, most under 12 inches—he would catch a couple of fat rainbows in the 20 inch range from the pond just a few steps from the camper door. To add insult to injury, he would be napping quite contentedly by the time I stumbled into the camper. I suffered all this gladly, mindful of similar sacrifices that had become part of Dad's legacy.

Dad's success fly-fishing never came anywhere near to matching the passion with which he engaged in the sport. The reason for this was simple. The time and dedication required to become proficient at this enterprise is significant, especially if you are self-taught. There is a reason they call this approach "trial and error," and Dad had experienced his share of both. To be honest, you have to be a little selfish to become a decent fly-fisherman. In fact, my informal observations have led me to conclude that, all else aside, selfishness and success in this sport are directly proportional. Incidentally, this explains why most good fly-fishermen maintain "catch and release" relationships with the women in their lives.

Dad had his vices, but selfishness was not one of them. Somewhere along the way he made a choice, likely subconscious, that he would rather introduce people to the sport and watch them enjoy it than become proficient at it himself. So, instead of sneaking off alone, he made it a habit to bring others along to share in the intoxicating pursuit of trout, and the serenity of their heavenly habitat. Though he was hardly an outgoing person, he recognized that having a brotherhood with which he could share his passion richened the experience. He became very proficient at this type of evangelism, and I was but one of many beneficiaries of his sacrifice.

Though we took it for granted then, we had the rare fortune of being raised within walking distance of the better part of our entire cousinhood during most of the time we were growing up. Mom and Dad had close relationships with their siblings, so there was a good bit of informal exchange of children, and we never had to work very hard to put together a gang—a positive term in those days—ready for adventure. Naturally, Dad found a ready-made pool of recruits for the Brotherhood among these cousins.

I learned only recently that Dad continued this practice even after I was grown and gone from the family home. When my son, Ryan, was a child he loved nothing more than spending a few days with Grandmother and Granddad in Gruver. Mom ran a preschool out of their home, and several of my cousin's children attended it. Apparently, Dad would wait until naptime, then "kid-nap" Ryan and his kin to take them fishing. To add a little excitement, he made it seem to them like this was all done under the radar and that even Grandmother did not know what they were doing. Forbidden fish, like fruit, are all the sweeter.

The eldest among our merry band of cousins was Barry. Dad had introduced Barry's father, Uncle Les, to trout fishing in the Rockies back in the '50s when they were courting the Ayres sisters. It did not stick with Les, but Barry would fall hard. He was two years my senior, and had become somewhat of a trail-blazer. He seemed to stay at least two years ahead of the curve in a community where, by the age of 12, all the boys were driving and working full time in the summer.

By the time I got my first Red Ryder BB gun, Barry was hunting pheasant with a 12 gauge. While I was seeing how far I could ride a wheelie on my bicycle, Barry was roaring around town on a 250cc dirt bike that, he claimed, could climb a telephone pole if you could stay on it. By the time I learned how to put gas in a car, Barry was overhauling irrigation motors on his dad's farm. Barry, it turns out, had inherited I.W.'s gift for carpentry as well, and would eventually become a top-notch framer, of homes that is. All this made Barry a rather independent and adventurous individual who is apt, as you will learn, to get me in over my head.

Dad's evangelistic efforts among the cousins had its downside. Once hooked, we were dependent on one of the dads to get us to the local catfish hole of choice every Sunday afternoon. We were merciless in our persistence, and ruined many a coveted Sunday afternoon nap with our pestering. The plotting would usually start during Sunday school, where we would pick out a "straggler" among the herd of fathers—one who would be too tired to put up much of a fight. If this failed, and we could not get any cooperation, we might start loading our gear in a truck as if it were understood that someone had agreed to take us, hoping whoever it was would not have the heart to disappoint us.

All of this changed when Cousin Barry inherited Uncle Will's blue '58 Chevy pickup. Now the world—of local catfish, anyway—was our oyster. We could go as far as we wanted…as long as we made it back for Sunday evening church services at six o'clock. We usually did, though not always with enough time to clean up properly. We turned more than a few blue-haired heads in our day as the smell of catfish and chicken liver is very difficult to get out from under your fingernails, and not exactly the aroma that puts you in the mood to worship the Almighty.

By the fall of 1999, Barry had heard all the secondhand fishing stories he could stomach, and decided to join us on our annual trip. No matter where we planned to go, we always found it difficult to get past Tolby Campground, at the head of Cimarron Canyon, and could not resist spending at least a night or two at that storied and enchanting site.

Dad, Brian, and I settled into the pop-up, while Cousin Barry, an established construction framer by this time, chose to go solo—erecting his tent fully square with the mountain and level with the tools of his trade. He had to dig through them anyway to find his fishing gear. The pop-up would have slept one more, but trailblazers don't like to encroach on established settings. Besides, there had been some bear trouble at the campground that summer, and Barry reasoned that, since all the meals were to be cooked in the pop-up, and the canvas was saturated with 30 years of fried food odor, he might be safer in his tent.

Unfortunately, and often to their own undoing, bears that inhabit forests near campgrounds sometimes find themselves irresistibly drawn in by the prospect of an easy meal. They quickly learn that garbage containers, coolers, and occasionally even the pockets of unfortunate campers contain all sorts of goodies that are hard to come by in their natural habitat. When it's time to fatten up for winter, they can become quite a nuisance, to the point of becoming dangerous. Experienced bears know that the Plexiglas windows of a pickup camper are easily dispensed with, and we were hearing tales of such shenanigans as we set up camp.

As a precaution, Barry announced he would sleep with Sluggo, his 38 ounce framing hammer, under his pillow. Barry is a big guy taking after the long and lanky Uncle Les, and once he became proficient in construction (ahead of the curve, of course), he realized that standard framing hammers did not pack all the punch he was capable of commanding. This slowed him down, which he found unacceptable. To overcome this handicap, he procured an oversized hammer and replaced the standard handle with a 24-inch ax handle, and Sluggo was born. Still, we questioned the sufficiency of this weapon in dealing with a hungry black bear. We were then treated to an impromptu demonstration of Barry's hammer-wielding prowess.

"Have you ever seen me drive a number eight nail?" he asked, with his classic, "I know something you don't chuckle." "Tap to set,"—the picnic table served nicely—"and...Wham! It's in!" Not through the wood in the two inch direction, mind you—that would be easy—but into the side of the lumber where the entire three and one half inch length of the nail disappeared in a flash. We learned that he often used this demonstration to inspire, or intimidate as the need demanded, members of his framing crew.

The bear stories had fueled Dad's PISD and put him on edge. Actually, he stayed pretty close to the edge most of the time anyway. What made Brian and I even more uneasy was that Dad had a tendency to fight unseen enemies in his sleep. On one occasion, years ago, as Uncle Les tells it, the tranquility of the night was shattered by a disturbance, which, upon investigation, turned out to be Dad hacking away at the brush with his trusty army surplus machete. Inquiry revealed that he was in the process of putting down a lion that he insisted had taken cover there. He did not remember a thing the next morning, of course.

At some point, as Dad aged, he must have lost confidence in his ability to wield that machete, for in its place under his mattress he kept a loaded J.C. Higgins, model-60, semi-automatic 12-gauge shotgun. He subscribed to the theory, common among hunters, that the gun you know is loaded is less dangerous than the one you think might not be. This brought him great comfort, despite the fact that "Rusty," as we affectionately referred to the gun, had been oxidizing in his bedroom closet since it was last fired during the pheasant season of 1978. Not only did he find security in Rusty, but since his mattress was composed of only three inches of light foam, the bulge made sleeping very uncomfortable. This thereby insured that he maintained the mean edge one needs to survive in the wilderness.

To Dad's credit, I should mention that he once purchased mace as a safer, more camper-friendly means of protection. He was quite proud of this high-tech addition to his arsenal, and insisted on treating me to a demonstration. He began with an explanation of how, according to an article he had read, one was to lay a fog of pepper spray in the air between himself and the charging enemy, be it a bear, or another disgruntled camper. He must have bought the spray at the close of the previous season, because, when he backed off and pressed the trigger, nothing more than a couple of drops of the irritant dribbled out of the nozzle and down onto his hand. Knowing that this was the kind of thing that really irritated Dad, I tried to lighten the mood.

"Am I supposed to hold the bear down while you dribble that into his eye?" I joked. He failed to see the humor in my response, and, while winding up to bean me with the would-be dispenser, slung a couple of drops into his eye. He added a few new moves and some fresh lyrics to the SOB shuffle that day.

Brian was uptight about the bear situation as well. Of course, Dad picked up on this, and sought, as was his nature, to intensify that anxiety with all sorts of bear tales, and quite a few well-timed grunting and scratching sounds.

"Did you boys hear that?" He would ask in mock fright. "Brian, why don't you go see what that was?"

I was not as concerned, since I had learned that if you put your food in the cab of a vehicle and clean up after yourself, the danger is minimal. Besides, most of us carry far more scars from encounters with other people than have ever been inflicted by wildlife in the whole history of camping. I was further comforted by the knowledge, which I kept to myself, that Brian had sat on a melted s'more earlier in the evening and had a big blob of Hershey's chocolate on his jeans. I figured he would therefore receive priority treatment should an unwelcomed guest pay us a visit—survival of the fittest, you understand.

Brian and I slept in one wing of the pop-up, while Dad occupied what you might call the "captain's quarters" on the other end. His berth overlooked the "kitchen table," and by dark, the pork rinds and Vienna sausages had been cleared off to make room for four or five Coleman lanterns. Dean's philosophy was that you could never have too many lanterns, and that if you had them, they might as well be lit. He was a hopeless insomniac, and, at home, he spent most of his nights in a recliner with his face about two feet from the TV. Apparently, the snowy static and white noise that resulted when the station signed off, as they did back in the days before all night infomercials, provided the ambience he needed for sleep.

As near as we could figure, five lanterns burning on the table must have simulated this environment for him. He would diligently tend each lantern through the course of the night, re-pressurizing and refueling them via the familiar thumb and forefinger pumping action that all real campers must master, and which he had tried in vain to teach us. By the end of the trip, Dad's face looked like Gary Cooper's in High Noon. We referred to this unique skin tone as "Coleman bronze." You see the color all the time nowadays on women, especially in the dead of winter. The extra fuel for the lanterns was stored in gallon containers in the cubbyholes beneath the seats of the camper, along with Dean's ammunition, in a quantity that caused me far more concern than the possibility of a marauding bear.

One lantern was placed strategically on the picnic table just outside the camper door so we could see what was coming to eat us. It also served as a harassment prop. Knowing that Brian was not about to set foot outside the camper until well after sunup, Dad would say, "Hey, Brian. I think that lantern is getting dim. Why don't you go out there and give it a few pumps."

The tension this night proved justified. At about 10 o'clock, we heard a loud commotion from the other side of the campground and subsequently learned that a bear was on the prowl. Someone—thankfully not Dad—fired a gun, and sent Cimarron, as the bear was dubbed, scurrying back into the brush. This, combined with Dad's ruthless tendency for practical jokes, meant that no one wanted to be the first in the camper to nod off.

Barry, who has the ability to fall asleep within seconds under any circumstances—I have timed him and his record is mere seconds from lucid conversation to loud snoring—was sawing away contently in the distance, none the wiser.

There was talk of pulling one on "Ol' Barry," as Dad was fond of calling him. The "bull-bear call" was a blood curdling sound effect Dad had developed years ago for just these kinds of circumstances, and he had used it to free the bladders of most of his camping compatriots at one point or another. Two things stopped him this night. One was the possibility of being on the receiving end of a blow from Sluggo. The other was the prospect of a 50-foot trip through the darkness where poetic justice might have brought the practical joker face to face with the real thing.

We talked bear strategies into the wee hours of the night. I tried to break the monotony by sharing some fascinating and highly useful information about the mating habits of the cased caddis fly. Coincidentally, it must have been about this time that we drifted off to sleep.

The next thing I knew, I was startled to semiconsciousness by loud clunking and shuffling at the other end of the trailer. The first thing I saw when my eyes popped open was Dad, landing on both feet with a thud, in the middle of the camper. Somehow, he had vaulted the length of the table and cleared the maze of lanterns. When he hit the floor, he started stomping and shuffling toward the door of the camper, in a kind of Riverdance fashion, shouting, "You Bear! Shoo, Shoo, Shoo!" Reflecting back later, I had to point out to him that, for someone who invented the bull-bear call, "You Bear! Shoo!" seemed a little lame.

Brian exploded from his sleeping bag, having no idea whether he was under attack or merely the object of some of Dad's orneriness, and let go with a quick volley of profanity. I thought it was probably some prank or one of Dad's dreams, but when I threw back the canvas, I saw a large black bear butt disappear into the brush not ten feet from my wing, and moving in the general direction of Barry's tent! That was the last sleep any of us got that night, Barry excluded, of course. Dad was the first to regain his composure, suggesting that Brian should "Go check on Ol' Barry. Oh, and prime the lantern while you're out there."

The next morning we found muddy paw prints on the pickup window, left when the bear stood to scope out the contents of the cab, mere feet from Dad's wing of the pop up. Had the bear turned and leaned the other way… well, in the words of Jerry Clower, we would have had to "shoot in there amongst 'em" to give one of them some relief. Barry had not heard or seen anything of the bear, though he had found Dad's "You Bear!" soft shoo, and Brian's blue accompaniment quite entertaining.

Chapter 10

Saved by the CLAW!

By the evening of the next day, following the "You Bear! Shoo!" incident, as it came to be known, Brian had worked himself into an anxious state. Of course, Dad was right there to egg it on, "City flesh is more tender than rural and is considered a delicacy among more sophisticated bears." By the time Barry and I returned from our afternoon assault on the river, Brian's mind was made up. He followed the sun over the pass and was

117

ensconced comfortably in a motel room in Eagle Nest, six miles from camp, by dark. Dad had ferried him over, and the situation created something new for him to worry about. He did not like the idea of Brian, who was 34 at the time, being in that motel room alone. Dad convinced himself that Brian was in more danger alone in civilization than I would be alone in the pop-up with a bear. In Dad's thinking, bears are predictable. They act like animals. But humans are often less than humane. You never know what they're going to do! To understand his logic, you have to know where Dad came from.

His father, Babe, died when Dad was only seven. Pamomma, as we referred to his mom, Ona, often said, "Once was enough," and never remarried. Dad, the oldest of three siblings, found his male role models, from that point on, in coaches and drill sergeants. His class motto, which he was very proud of and considered the most stunning piece of poetry ever penned, was: "Tough as nails, hard as bricks, we're the class of '56." He developed a hard-edged, "get the first lick in" attitude toward society, which he tried in vain to pass on to at least one of his three sons, who became, respectively, a pastor, a counselor, and a hair stylist.

Whenever we came home from school with news that there was a new guy in our class, his consistent reply was, "Did you whip his ass?" In his mind, if a stranger approaches you, odds are he is up to no good, and you should thus be prepared for a fight. If you don't understand the first words out of his mouth, the proper response is a withering "Screw you!" Since Dad was hard of hearing—he had not heard the first words out of anyone's mouth in 15 years—this could be somewhat embarrassing for the family if, for instance, someone was asking for directions. We became quite adept at running interference and one of us usually managed to get between him and any approaching stranger. Only close family members knew that this posture of Dad's was mostly bluff. He wanted fear to be the first impression he left with people and he was usually successful in that endeavor.

So, in Dad's mind, it was clear that Brian was much more vulnerable in that motel with all those strangers than I would be alone in the pop-up. After an hour or so of fretting, he announced his decision, "I'd better go stay with Brian. I don't want him to be in that motel room by himself." Since we could not leave the camper unattended, and did not want to give up our prime site, I was left to guard the rig. He gave me some last minute instructions on how to pressurize the lanterns and which ones might need new mantles by morning. I dutifully pretended to understand his instructions, and then he was off, leaving me in a camper that, by this time, smelled to a bear like home fries and bacon sandwiches with a side order of ripe fisherman.

Even with Rusty under my pillow, and Sluggo guarding my six, I was not eager to hit the sack under those conditions, so I lured Barry over with some of Mom's homemade cinnamon rolls. We had work to do anyway.

Barry and I had long ago talked ourselves into believing that we were either one fly, or one technical tweak away from fly-fishing's sanctum sanctorum—that tomorrow, the doors of fly-fishing mastery would swing open wide for us and that we would enter a magical world where every cast was rewarded by a rod-arcing hook-up. This delusion is common among fly-fishermen and is so powerful that even poignant and potentially crippling memories of disappointing fly-fishing experiences have very short lives. In fact, by the time the waders dry, these memories are usually fully repressed, banished to some impenetrable vault in the subconscious. If they ever resurface, they are viewed as having happened to some other poor fellow who did not know what he was doing. I do not claim to understand the physiological mechanics of this self-induced brain washing, but without it, there would not be many of us on the stream.

So, as was our custom, we passed the evening tying a few more "can't miss" flies, to replace the "can't miss" flies we had lost that afternoon; turns out "can't miss" applies as much or more to trees and rocks than it does to fish. To break things up, I occasionally read aloud some poignant passage from my portable library of fishing magazines. I tried to stay away from "how to" articles at night since they always introduce the reader to tie a couple of new "can't miss" flies, which, of course, means another two hours at the vice and usually results in nothing more than a bit more variety in the streamside foliage in the end. At least Barry was interested, or he pretended to be, as long as the cinnamon rolls held out.

Somewhere around 11 p.m., Barry returned from the out-house facilities with some exciting news. He had encountered an ashen-faced fellow along the way who claimed that a bear had gotten itself trapped in the dumpster. The lids are designed to be "bear proof" by means of a latch that catches when the lid is closed and requires some dexterity to release. This is supposed to frustrate the bear, who, lacking opposable thumbs and our advanced powers of logic, cannot gain entrance. Personally, I wouldn't mind the bears raiding the trashcans if it kept them out of my pockets, but I was not consulted. Apparently, Cimarron had evolved some means of getting around the latch problem—this is always the danger in toying with nature. Maybe the "You Bear! Shoo!" display Dad had employed the evening before had motivated the bear to try the dumpster first this time.

Barry and I had trouble imagining how a bear could have

gotten into the dumpster and managed to close the lid on itself. We were dubious, and, with the latch secure, we decided it would be safe for us to investigate this matter for ourselves. Sometimes, city folk let their imaginations run away with them. "It's probably just a raccoon or something," I said as I kicked the dumpster. Something not unlike a muffled bull-bear call answered from within. This made our neck hairs stand on end, stiff as the hackle on an Adams, well tied from a grade-one rooster cape.

"It would be just like Dean to sneak back over here and pull a prank like this," I suggested. "We would feel pretty stupid if we called the park ranger and Dean was in the dumpster. And if he got in trouble, he would probably blame us and might make more trouble for us than the bear!"

Barry agreed and added, "Yeh. We'd better make sure." We could open the lid about two inches with the latch still caught and decided, after some debate, that this would be the best option. Barry worked the nail-pulling end of Sluggo under the lid and pried it open while I focused the flashlight into the crack. I had seen Dad get ferocious at times, but he did not have brown eyes, and they were not as far apart as the animal that was looking back at me. As for the disposition, well, it was a toss-up.

Though the latch had given us enough courage to give the situation a closer look, the face to face encounter prompted a hasty retreat to a more strategic location where we caught our breath and planned our next move. We considered alerting the campground manager. But this position is usually given to some retired couple in exchange for a free camping spot for the summer, plus they are rarely available for real crises. Of course, if you are three minutes late with the day's toll for your camping slot, you can count on a visit. We had no idea how to get in contact with anyone from the forest service at that time of night, so we decided to call 911.

"Do you know the 911 number in New Mexico?" I asked, still a bit shaken.

Reception was poor, but Barry was able to get through by standing on top of his truck and replacing his four inch cell phone antenna with his fly rod. I don't know if that really helped, but it was an interesting sight. We settled back and tried to imagine what the response might be. What would be the protocol for such a situation? Maybe the police would alert the forest service and they would transport the dumpster somewhere safe and free the bear. Or, maybe some Steve Irwin type would fly in and save the day... "Crikey! Sounds like Ursa mighta goit himself hopped-up on some leftovah powdahed doughnuts!" We might even be interviewed on the Nature Channel! The air crackled with excitement.

Within 20 minutes, a black-and-white arrived leading us to conclude that New Mexico police must undergo some kind of special training for these kinds of situations. We were soon proven wrong. A couple more patrol cars arrived, and, after they had assembled what they deemed to be appropriate force, they began their analysis. Something about this particular circumstance must have been different from any they had encountered in training. They repeatedly circled the dumpster, occasionally cracking the lid to reassure themselves of what they had seen, and convened back at the command post to discuss strategy. We were not allowed close enough to hear what they were plotting. This really bothered Barry, since he tends to have very firm ideas about how most problems ought to be handled. At one point, they consulted a manual, and I can only assume that they were trying to determine whether they had enough Taser volts among them to disable a bear.

Finally, one of the officers rummaged around in the trunk of his squad car for something. "What's he after?" wondered Barry. "a trap… a tranquilizer gun… a rifle…a leash?" What he finally brought into the glaring lights of the cruiser was a three foot strand of wire that looked a lot like an opened coat hanger. We could hardly believe our eyes as their plan unfolded. The officer secured the wire to the lid of the dumpster and walked around behind, holding the loose end of the wire. He took a moment in which he seemed to be engaged in some sort of mental preparations, somewhat like a karate expert who is about to break a stack of bricks with his forehead. He then signaled a compatriot who freed the latch and beat a hasty retreat to one of the cruisers.

Once the officer behind the dumpster had worked up sufficient courage, he slowly raised the lid by means of his strand of wire. We learned later that what looked to us like a coat hanger bent straight was, in fact, a CLAW—Critter Liberation Attainment Wire; standard issue for New Mexico's finest, and illegal for the private citizen—who would not likely pay the $735 price tag anyway. As another "safety" feature, the lids of these dumpsters can only raise a couple of feet and must be held open. For the brave trooper, this meant that he was going to have to hang on to the wire until Cimarron cleared the rim. This is where the plan fell apart.

The trooper had chosen a CLAW that was too short to put a comfortable distance between himself and the bear. As a result, his iron will and incredible courage abandoned him when he saw Cimarron's head rising cautiously into the light, and he released the wire. By this time, the bear's head was completely above the rim so that the weighty lid, once free, descended with a thud on his crown and sent him grunting back to the bottom of the receptacle. He made several angry laps, rocking the dumpster

123

ominously from within, before he settled back down.

The officers retrieved the brave CLAW wielder from a nearby tree, and he sat out the rest of the ordeal. Personally, I would not be too comfortable with this "trial and error" approach, given the potential consequences on the error side of the equation, but the men in blue were clearly not ready to concede defeat. After several minutes, they settled on what can only be described as a bold strategy. Well, it could be described another way, but let's give them the benefit of the doubt. We watched in disbelief as another officer climbed atop the dumpster and was handed the CLAW. I have heard it said that hunters use elevated deer stands because deer "never look up" since they are rarely preyed upon from above. Maybe the same is true of bears. Who were we to question these brave officers?

For whatever reason, they had determined that this position, four feet above the ground, provided the new operator of the CLAW the safety buffer he needed. For our part, we took a couple of steps closer to Barry's truck, just in case things, particularly the bear, went south. Barry laid out the terms in his classic cut-and-dried way, "If we make it into the truck and the bear chases them this way, do not open the door to let them in. That would only create more casualties. I will leave Sluggo out here in case they need it." Barry had been through some sort of disaster training back home as a volunteer EMT, so I was not in a position to argue. This was also Barry's way of tactfully letting me know that if I were too slow getting into the truck, he would have no choice but to lock me out as well, and that it was nothing personal.

Once the SWAT team had released the latch, each member but one assumed a position very near the door of his police cruiser. The CLAW operator slowly raised the lid. Cimarron was a little bit tentative this time. He did a couple of slow pokes just above the rim to see if the sky was going to fall again. When he decided to make his move, it was quite impressive.

I have heard that bears can move much faster than their clumsy looking anatomy might suggest. By the time I realized he was out, he had already hit the ground in front of the dumpster and executed a 180 in a flash of fur. Fleeing the spotlights, he disappeared into the pines behind the dumpster before anyone could move. We speculated that the trooper atop the dumpster might have planned to dive in himself if the bear had decided to hang around. As it was, he stood paralyzed, hand frozen to the CLAW having realized two things: bears really can move faster than their clumsy looking anatomy might suggest, and, sometimes, your bowels move before your feet can.

Chapter 11

The Relativity of Comfort

With fly fishing, as with any activity that brings such satisfaction, there exists the compulsion to evangelize. I choose this term because it conveys the seriousness and urgency with which we often find ourselves proselytizing friends and acquaintances into our sport of choice. While I have had my share of challenges bringing trout to net, I must confess that I have been utterly skunked when it comes to converting friends and family to the long rod. In fact, my experiences fly-fishing, whether witnessed firsthand or conveyed through word of mouth, tend to drive people away from the sport rather than toward it.

Recently, I had the privilege of fishing a honey hole of a bass pond in eastern Oklahoma with its property owner. After watching me work myself into a lather with two hours of fly-casting that yielded not a single fish as he hauled in bass after bass on a balsa minnow, he inquired, "Why do you have to do everything the hard way?"

His question left me speechless. For a brief moment, I saw the venture from his point of view and wondered if he did not have a point. "This really is the 'hard way,'" I thought. "Why am I doing this?" This is a question that a fly-fisherman should never entertain! If ever allowed to take root in the psyche, it will grow like a bramble. Every time you find yourself climbing a tree to retrieve a fly, sitting on the bank untangling a leader, stripping down to your underwear to dry your clothes after an unplanned swim, or casting five feet short of a rise form on the lake despite your best double-haul, this noxious thought will sprout new branches. If left unchecked, it can utterly destroy an angler. Fly-fishermen thus consumed are often seen sitting on the bank of some river, a look of profound despondency etched on the face, rod in lap, staring blankly at the water and muttering, "Why?"

Fortunately for me, a five pound bass took a swipe at my deer hair popper before the question had a chance to sink in and I was merrily on my way once again. A little intermittent reinforcement goes a long, long way!

Though my evangelistic efforts have never succeeded, they have yielded some interesting incidents along the way. An unusually compact cluster of such events occurred during the You Bear! Shoo! Fall Fishing Extravaganza of 2000.

The "whys" very nearly crushed the life out of me that fall. In October of 2000, my dad passed away quite suddenly. In one cataclysmic moment, I lost a father, a fishing buddy, a friend, and a hero. Our most recent correspondence—which we had no idea would be our last—concerned the plans for that year's fishing trip. Suddenly, for me, camping and fishing seemed like anything but "livin'." I had no motivation to get back at it and I was certainly not in the mood to plan a solo outing. I honestly did not know what it would be like to go without him. I felt guilty even considering it. As far as I was concerned, the sport of fly-fishing died with Dad. "Why go to all that trouble?"

Cousin Barry came to the rescue. Barry had shared part of the '99 outing and had thus taken part in the "You Bear! Shoo!" incident that had given these trips their title. He is a perplexing blend of zany genius and is prone to twist off in the most unpredictable of directions at a whim. Once he gets his sights set on something, there is no stopping him. In fact, if you show the least bit of interest, he will insist you go along for the ride.

As I wrote this book, in fact, he had spent the last few months in his garage tinkering with a surplus water heater and a couple of 55-gallon barrels in which he intended to convert frying oil into fuel. He treated me to regular updates on the project. The most recent involved a demonstration showing how he titrates the raw oil to determine the quantity of fatty acids present.

After very nearly burning down his house, suffering a third degree oil scald on his thigh, and coming dangerously close to rendering himself a eunuch by the most painful means imaginable, Barry did indeed produce a batch of biodiesel that he successfully tested in his truck. Once the challenge was met, he lost interest and the enterprise was abandoned. When I am forced to reduce Barry's persona to words, I describe him as "Thomas Edison meets Kosmo Kramer."

By contrast, Dad and I were much less adventurous. Where Barry was capable of talking himself—and anyone around him—into almost anything, Dad and I were able to talk ourselves out of almost anything if we thought about it very long. Dad kept an eye on Ol' Barry, as he called him, and kept me abreast of his latest enterprises even after I left home—adventure by proxy, you might call it. These tales typically began, "Ol' Barry came by the other day…"

Less than a week after we returned from our trip in '99, I got one of those calls from Dad. Apparently, our experience had inspired Ol' Barry—and when Ol' Barry gets inspired, we have all learned to take shelter because there is no telling what is about to be affected, erected, neglected, demolished, or legislated.

"Ol' Barry called me the other day from the showroom of the annual outdoor exposition at the Amarillo Civic Center," Dad began. I knew what was coming because Ol' Barry had called me as well. Barry usually introduces his latest shenanigans with a baited question that does not provide the listener with nearly enough information to hazard even the vaguest guess at what he is doing. This puts Barry firmly in the driver's seat of the conversation, and the passenger at his mercy, as he slowly and deliberately divulges every savory morsel of fact and fiction that has captured his fancy.

"You will never guess where I am and what I have just done!" Barry began cryptically. I knew that the conversation could not move forward until I responded, but what do you say?

"You are in Tibet buying breeding stock for your Llama herd," I answered. My sarcasm, and any humor it contained, was summarily dismissed as irrelevant, a needless distraction to the tale at hand.

"No." responded Barry, not missing a beat. "I am at the outdoor exposition in Amarillo. You will never believe what I have just done." The pause that followed indicated that another response was expected.

"You bought a timeshare that allows you to stay in prime Cape Buffalo range for only $5 a night any time the buffalo are not there?" I jested.

"No," he shot back. "I already have one of those. I have just signed the papers for a 32-foot travel trailer. That is a foot longer than most of the camp slots in New Mexico," he chuckled. What might sound like a drawback to most was just another chance to stretch the envelope for Barry.

Apparently, while inspired by the concept of a yearly fishing trip, Barry could not imagine his 6' 4" frame ever finding peace in the confines of Uncle Dean's pop-up, assuming that he thought about that at all. It is more likely that he went to the show to salivate over fly rods, realized he could not afford one, and bought a travel trailer instead. That may not make any sense to you and me, but we are talking about Barry here. In addition to his degree in construction, Barry also earned a master's degree in creative justification somewhere along the way. In the time it takes a neuron to fire, he is capable of forging an airtight, unassailable—from his point of view—rationalization for virtually anything he wants to do or buy. Once he has convinced himself, selling the idea to any would-be detractors is merely a matter of patient condescension.

The hurdle he needed to clear in order to justify this purchase was this: financially speaking, 32 feet of travel trailer was quite a stretch for him, somewhere around 31.5 feet too much, to be precise. To make this fiscally feasible, he needed to spin what looked like a recreational extravagance as a shrewd investment.

This was no problem. Barry is a construction framer by trade and had been working several hours from home of late. This meant ferrying a crew back and forth, a waste of valuable time, or renting hotel rooms, which cut into an already slim profit margin. A travel trailer could house his crew and be written off as a business expense!

I am not sure how many nights the camper was actually used for business purposes. While 32 feet is more than enough room for two fly-fishermen, I would imagine that things felt a little cramped for a four- or five-man framing crew. They don't tend to return in the evening in quite as jolly a mood as fishermen, I'm sure, especially when constrained by Barry's restrictive bathroom regulations—of which the number one rule is no "number two" in the camper. Showers are scripted in detail and rehearsed to conserve hot water. You get one warning if you go long, then Barry shuts off the hot water.

Of course, Barry's shrewdness was not limited to matters of recreation or invention. It must have occurred to him that his crew, headed for the confines of a travel trailer instead of home, would have a vested interest in getting the project done in a timely fashion. Thus, they might work a little faster and maybe even a little later. These were two things for which Barry was always pressing.

These are not criticisms, mind you. In this case, I was to become a grateful beneficiary of Barry's powers of justification. For an outdoor enthusiast who wants to maintain at least the rudimentary comforts of home, a desire that grows exponentially with age, moving from a used, 16-foot pop-up to a new 32-foot travel trailer is not unlike winning the lottery.

I was informed that the first "You Bear! Shoo! Fall Fly-fishing Extravaganza" of the new millennium would be enjoyed in this castle on wheels. By this time, it was well broken in by the framing crew, and had housed Barry's family of five once or twice when the timeshare accommodations did not pan out. Cape Buffalo, Barry discovered, can be quite unpredictable!

For my part, I was alarmingly indifferent about making another foray into paradise. It was as if all the meaning had been drained from term "livin'." Barry had to pull out the big guns, in terms of emotional manipulation, to get me off high center. "What would your dad want?" He reasoned, and "We can't let the tradition he started die with him. It's our responsibility to carry on," and such.

This was one instance when I must admit that I am grateful for his shrewd stubbornness. I remind him, occasionally, that if it weren't for him, my fly rod would likely be nothing more than a wall ornament by now.

At any rate, with the death of my dad in mid-October, the trip got pushed back into early November. The weather at our favorite haunts high in the Rockies can be wintery by this time, but Barry assured us that this would be, "no problem." Among the amenities of the trailer, as minutely detailed by Barry to any who cared to listen and several who did not, was central heating.

In fact, the space and relative luxury were deemed to be more than two country boys can enjoy. Dad had a set the precedent for evangelism, so we invited Barry's dad, Les, and brother-in-law Ricky along for the fun. Uncle Les had been one of the privileged few who had been introduced to the pursuit of salmonids and the wondrous haunts they inhabit, by my dad. He is thus a charter member of The Brotherhood of Dean.

But Les never really got "hooked." He does not dislike fishing, and if you rig up a pole for him and drive him to the edge of a river, he will partake. However, if there is very much initiative at all required on his part, he will usually opt out. Newton proved that an object at rest will remain at rest unless acted upon by an outside force. In this case, Les was the object and Barry was the outside force. The "comforts of home" are what Barry finally promised, since this was what kept Les from overcoming the inertia that anchored him to his favorite recliner.

At this point in his life, Les was accustomed to three home-cooked, multicourse meals per day, many of which were delivered to him in his recliner by Aunt Sharon. This spared him the arduous eight foot trip to the kitchen table. Sharon was of the old school of wifery that is all but extinct these days. I won't say Les was spoiled, but I doubt that he has ever seen his iced tea glass go empty. I winced a little, during the planning stages of this trip, every time the phrase "comforts of home" was employed, knowing that Barry and Les had very different ideas about just what that meant.

As was our pattern, we were late getting off. We stopped to eat at an hour when Les would otherwise have been firmly ensconced in the Broyhill, tea glass at hand, dozing through the latest rerun of Bonanza. No one has ever had the heart to tell him that this show is not a documentary about ranching, and he tends to get a little cranky without his nightly dose of Hoss and Little Joe.

We chose a submarine sandwich joint for the first meal of the trip. Even as we pulled in, Barry predicted that Les, who was following us in Ricky's truck, would likely make a fuss of some kind about this choice. He explained that, until recently, his dad was unaware that food was prepared anywhere but in the kitchen at home, or at the diner at the local livestock auction. But we thought this represented a fair middle ground between what he was used to at home and what he would experience in the days to come.

True to form, the first words out of Les's mouth as we disembarked were, "Subway? What do they serve here?" Les is one of those people who can cram an incredible amount of bellyaching into very few words, the depth of frustration being conveyed primarily through his tone and facial expression. It's a hangdog, droopy look that says, "I'd rather be anywhere but here, doing anything but this, with anyone but you." We would become very familiar with this expression over the next three days. Barry, always up for a challenge, had it in the back of his mind that his dad would find, and maybe even express, a bit of joy at some point during this excursion. I could see right away that this was not going to happen at Subway!

Barry responded to Les's question, bracing himself for the inevitable complaint, "Sandwiches."

"Sandwiches?" drolled Les, in a tone that seemed to indicate that he was unfamiliar with the term. "And…?"

"That's it," I said. "Just sandwiches."

"Is that supposed to be a meal?" Les replied incredulously.

Explaining that these were no ordinary sandwiches to someone who had never had a sandwich seemed like a waste of energy.

Les was baffled by the process from the moment we walked in the door. He tried to sit down, and we informed him that he would have to order from the counter.

"Standing up?" He pouted.

Barry illustrated the process by ordering two 12-inch meatball sandwiches. He was not all that hungry, as we had been snacking on the road. When we were kids, he explained his ability to put away food—he ate cereal out of a two quart mixing bowl—this way: "You see, I have an invisible second stomach. When I get full, I mentally open a valve between the two, empty the first, and start over." His youthful metabolism, and the fact that all those calories were spread out over his large frame, left Barry a virtual beanpole despite his superhuman consumption habits. "I never met a pizza I could not conquer," he often boasted. Then middle age hit. He was 40 at the time of this particular trip, and had begun to notice that his second stomach, though still demanding its due portions, was becoming more and more visible.

Still reeling from the revelation that there is more than one kind of bread, Les moved on to the toppings. The sight of raw vegetables was a new experience for him as well, and one he found downright disturbing. Though the Barkleys tended a mean garden every summer back in Gruver, it was outside Les' purview. Traditionally, this was considered woman's work, as it was beneath the dignity of a man to till any piece of ground under 100 acres that required less than $200,000 worth of equipment. Thus, Les had never seen the raw fruit of the earth until it had been Betty-Crockered into a dish fit for a...well...fit for a Les. Though Aunt Sharon was expected to set forth voluminous quantities, she was by no means a slouch in terms of quality.

"What's all this?" Les asked, sporting his best hangdog expression and pointing at the vegetables, "Looks like rabbit fodder." When he finally made it to the table and unwrapped his sandwich, he stared at it as if he were unsure where to begin. "Look at all that bread!" he complained. It took us a few minutes to convince him that he had not been scammed, and that bread really was a critical component of the traditional sandwich. "But they gave me two heels," he whined, "and an empty cup! What in the world have you guys gotten me into? You guys are nuts!"

That was the first of many times we would hear that phrase in the next three days.

As we pulled out of the parking lot a few minutes later, we figured there was a 50-50 chance that Les would not continue with us. Barry had already suggested that the second vehicle, unnecessary since his was a super cab, was probably meant to serve as an escape pod if the going got too tough, and a meal of sandwiches, he assured me, was pushing the limits. We were a bit surprised, therefore, to see their headlights in the mirror as we headed West. As it turned out, the poor guy was thinking, "It can only get better from here on out."

Thus is the hope of many a fisherman.

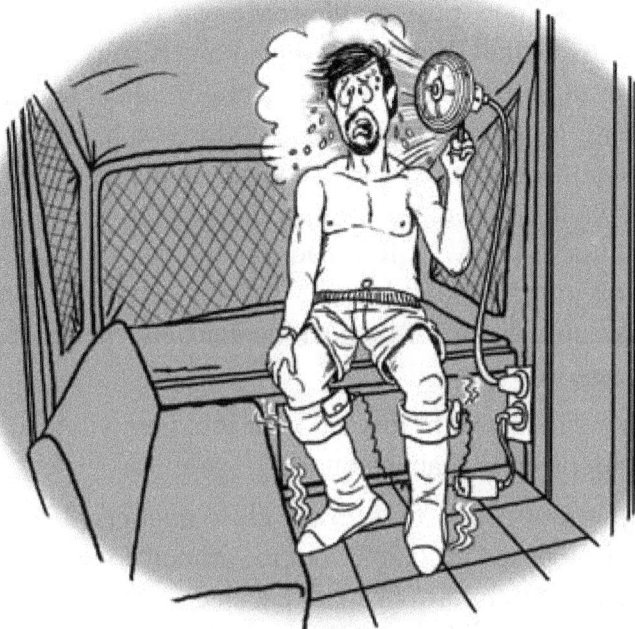

Chapter 12

Murphy Goes Camping

We arrived at our chosen campground, high up on the Cimarron, around midnight. At 9,000 feet, the November air had a healthy bite to it, and after a brief set-up, crisply directed by Barry, we clamored into the camper.

Now, for those not familiar with travel trailer dimensions, it should be noted that measurements like "32 feet" reflect exterior proportions, measured from bumper to bumper and always rounded up. Barry and Les are both 6'4", so the first thing that struck us was just how little usable space was left once we were all inside. The fact that Ricky and I are both vertically challenged did not seem to help much. Having spent considerable time and energy talking up the amenities and comforts to his dad, Barry was quick with words of reassurance meant to dispel the sense of claustrophobia that was registering on the faces of his guests. He commented that his crew of four had found the accommodations more than adequate, though I doubt that this conclusion was arrived at through any sort of democratic analysis. More likely, it was something like this:

Barry: "If you want to keep your job, you will find these accommodations more than adequate."

As the four of us stood in the close quarters, Les asked, "Where am I supposed to sleep?" looking around doubtfully. Barry had chosen not to inform his dad that sleep was something we considered optional, and engaged in only fitfully on these trips. The bunks were hidden in the corner, the couch folded out into a third bed, and the primary bed, the only one readily recognizable as such, occupied the "master bedroom." Les was informed that the couch would be his berth, to which he responded, "Oh Good! Where is the other half of me going to sleep?" I was beginning to get an idea why my sarcasm never seemed to break through to Barry.

The ceremonial lighting of the furnace was meant to be the first in a long line of demonstrations that would lead any rational person to agree with Barry's "all the comforts of home" assurances. He began with a detailed explanation of just how the heater worked, along with a set of guidelines about its proper use. As it turned out, Barry had a set of guidelines for the most efficient and pragmatic employment of most every facet of this particular model of Sprinter Camper.

Les cut him short on this one, "This is interesting, but my feet are turning blue. Can you just light the thing?"

Barry conceded, and proudly provided play-by-play as we heard the click of the thermostat followed by the whoosh of the furnace and, finally, the hum of the fan as the system came to life. Soon, warm air was blowing from each of the three floor vents along the center walkway. Barry was so proud, I half expected him to start handing out cigars as we settled in for the night.

It was not long, however, before we noticed that the welcomed warm-up did not seem to be keeping pace with the falling temperature outside. We each took our turn over various vents, trying to convince ourselves that the air circulating through the unit was warmer than we were. By that time, however, we were getting chilly. Any air above freezing would have felt warm to us, but we soon had to admit what investigation quickly confirmed—the fan was still running, but the furnace was not.

"That's odd," said Barry. "I have never had this trouble before." He shut down the system and restarted it, demanding silence as we listened for the telltale whoosh. There was none. He swapped out some fuses and tried again. No whoosh. He checked the gas connections, using a lit match, a much more dramatic leak indicator than the standard soap and water method, and tried again. No whoosh. He knew he was on thin ice in more ways than one. So far, the promise of heat had been the only redeeming aspect of the trip for Les, and Barry knew he would never hear the end of it if things did not turn around right quick. He might not hear the end of it anyway. Not to worry, Barry had never met a mechanical problem he could not lick...until this particular night!

It was well past midnight, and someone suggested we hunker down for the night and make the best of it since this was clearly not going to be an easy fix. Someone was ignored. Barry dropped to the "kitchen floor," his head in by his "bedroom" and his knees in Les's, and began tinkering with the heating unit. I, as usual, held the light for him while Ricky grumbled inarticulately and fetched the various tools Barry called for. In the back and forth to the truck, what little warmth we had accumulated was soon swept out into the frigid night, where the temperature was now into the lower 20s. We knew this because Barry brought a thermometer to keep track of the temperature outside to remind us just how fortunate we were to be in his trailer. This plan was backfiring on him.

Unoccupied, Les now monitored the thermometer, and was reporting each precious degree that slipped away. Between reports, he was free to comment ad nauseam about the futility of this undertaking, and the growing discomfort he was experiencing.

It was not enough to be outright discouraging, either. Les was experimenting with new ways of predicting absolute failure. This was not unusual and it had characterized the working relationship Barry and his dad had developed while farming together. It was a strange synergistic effort in which Barry had learned to feed off of Les' negativity, turning it into motivation. The more doubt Les expressed, the more determined Barry became. In a twisted way, Barry owed his mechanical ability to his dad's stubborn pessimism. In this case, however, it set in motion a vicious cycle that made for one long night!

We were not far into the process when we began to get a sense of just how creative engineers have become in packing all those amenities into the relatively small confines of a camper. Convenient servicing of any appliance had been sacrificed at every turn in favor of space. It was clear that they did not intend for the owner to do any maintenance while he or she was on the road, much less at 9,000 feet in November! But they, like most of us, had not anticipated Barry. It was also clear that they probably did not hire very many technicians of Barry's physical stature. The final assembly must surely be done by Oompa Loompas.

Barry could not even get a satisfactory diagnosis without completely removing the unit. After a good bit of blind screwing and several more trips in and out of the trailer, he had the beast in the camper floor where he could bring the full brunt of his mechanical skills to bear on it. Motivated by Les's steady stream of negativity, Barry had the heater humming again in short order.

A less experienced complainer would have been silenced by Barry's success, but Les was up to the challenge. "Well, good." He drolled. "Maybe the ice will have melted off my chin by breakfast. It's only 30 minutes away!"

Unfortunately, lying in the middle of the floor, as it was, the unit would soon asphyxiate us if we ran it that way. By now, it was past two in the morning. Barry, remembering a formula from high school chemistry, calculated that given the square footage of the trailer, we would survive if we did not sleep past six a.m. He was a little uncertain about the margin of error, though, since the air temperature was a variable that could not be precisely determined. He assured us that he could build an effective, albeit rudimentary, CO detector with equipment on hand. This sounded a little risky to the rest of us, and we decided it would be worth the time to put the heating unit back in its space.

Now that Barry was familiar with the set-up, he was able to accomplish the task in relatively short order. He rose confidently and turned to the thermostat. We heard the fan whir, and waited for the ignition whoosh of the burner…and waited…and waited…. Out of desperation, we convinced ourselves that perhaps we had not been able to hear it over the periodic complaints of Les, who was no longer heeding Barry's demands for silence during the would be "whoosh" phase. We each took a vent and tested the air for warmth again, to no avail.

I had seen this look on Barry's face before. The word determination simply does not capture the expression. Of course, Les was adding fuel to the fire, or lack thereof, stoking the coals of Barry's resolve by the minute. We each added another layer of clothes as Barry dug in. This time it was a loose wire—one that could not be tightened without removing the unit once again. And so it was, in and out, up and down, back and forth, gritch and moan.

By three a.m., the heater was in the aisle and working like a charm. By 3:30, it was back in its compartment…and not working at all. The camper batteries were running low, and Barry decided that we would attack the recalcitrant unit in the morning.

Meanwhile, we were faced with a dilemma. We could light the burners on the stove and fend off the chill to some degree, thus risking carbon monoxide poisoning, or we could freeze to death. Barry recalculated our odds based on the new source of carbon monoxide, and was convinced that we had at least four hours before saturation compromised our mental processes. Les said that he was certain that Barry's were already compromised. We decided to light only three of the four burners, just to be "safe."

We soon learned that this method of heating creates some pronounced thermoclines within a camper. At floor level, where the somewhat sensitive little piggies reside, the air temperature was a brisk 22 degrees. Waist high, it settled somewhere between 30 and 33 degrees, depending on one's height. At mid-chest, for Ricky and I, which was about belly button level for Les and Barry, things were comfortable at about 68 degrees. Another six inches, at the height of an average camper's head, however, it was downright warm, pushing 85 degrees. For the two taller members of our party, the temperature at nose level, up near the ceiling, was near 100 degrees and devoid of any humidity; great for drying waders but hell on the nasal membranes.

The obvious solution was to go to bed. In a prone position, the temperature from head to toe was relatively constant. Three of the beds were knee level, which was about 28 degrees. Unfortunately, the fourth bed, Ricky's, was the top bunk, less than two feet from the ceiling, and a toasty 95 degrees. Barry assured us that carbon monoxide produced over the burners was going to rise because of the heat, making the occupant of the top bunk first in line for possible asphyxiation. I, being a light sleeper anyway, was to check his breathing every 30 minutes or so since Ricky would be the first to show symptoms of carbon monoxide poisoning. If his breathing became labored, or ceased, that would let the rest of us know that we needed to get some fresh air.

Ricky, who is not much of a talker and had said nothing up to this point, felt compelled to complain that his status as an in-law was resulting in unfair treatment. This, we informed him, was merely coincidental, and that he was exhibiting paranoia typical of his East Coast roots. In fact, he was the only one among us who had the gymnastic ability to launch himself through the narrow opening into the top bunk without going through the ceiling. So, each of us settled into his assigned spot to chatter, or broil, as it were, through the rest of the night.

We had been down less than five minutes when we were startled by an excited, "I've got it!" from the master bedroom. "Yeh, I've got it too," said Les. "It's called frostbite!"

"No, no," responded Barry. "I know what is wrong with the heater. I figured it out in a dream!"

"Bull!" mumbled Les. "You guys are nuts!"

Honestly, I was not all that surprised. I knew that Barry was capable of falling asleep almost instantly, and that he often jumped straight into the dream phase. It was common for him to be carrying on a conversation one minute and having a dream the next. We could be talking about where we might fish tomorrow, and suddenly he would shake the trailer as he set the hook on his dream trout. In fact, this was so common that I once timed him out of curiosity. His record, from the point of cogent conversation to waking himself through dream-state flailing, was 22 seconds, repeating this process as many as four or five times in as many minutes.

Apparently, when presented with a baffling problem, Barry's mind continues to hammer away as he sleeps. I know this is hard to believe, but I had seen it first hand. We were in high school when Rubik's Cube first hit the market. Everybody had one, and we were all in various stages of tinkering with them, each hoping to be the first in the community to restore all six sides of the cube to their respective colors. The further one got, the more complicated things became since each successive move must be made without disturbing what had already been accomplished.

Barry hacked away at the problem with his characteristic stubbornness and developed a system that allowed him to complete the top side, the middle row, and four pieces on the bottom. This left only the corners to set right, which was proving to be quite a challenge. He was struggling with them one day when he slipped into one of his famous naps, during which he dreamed the solution.

"You will never guess what I have done!" I heard as I picked up the phone.

"You put wings on your motorcycle, and now it flies?" I

offered.

"No, that is not mechanically feasible—I tried," he answered. "I have beaten the Rubik's Cube!"

I was skeptical, so he invited me over for a demonstration. He put the cube right down to the last corners and said, "Now, this is what I dreamed: quarter turn, half turn, half turn, quarter turn, full turn, quarter turn, half turn, half turn and, voila!" My jaw dropped. He handed me the cube and instructed me to jumble it. As I handed it back to him, he grinned, and snickered, "Time me." The cube was a blur of colors as he began spinning various planes on their axis. In just under three minutes, the cube was righted again. He made me hang around until he could do it in under two minutes, then he taught me the moves.

It was neither the Rubik's Cube nor puzzling trout that had infiltrated his dreams this night, but the mysterious malfunction of the heater. Barry not only falls asleep like an apoplectic, but his sleep seems to be a lot more effective than that of an average person. It's a family trait, actually. A stint of 30 minutes sleep for a Barkley is the equivalent of roughly six hours for the average person. They will keep you up 'til three a.m. playing dominoes and then expect a full day's work out of you by six in the morning. So it was that Barry felt quite refreshed and was ready to attack the heater again. Only through threat of mutiny were we able to persuade him to wait until morning.

When it comes to sleep, I happen to be an anti-Barkley. It takes me about two hours to drift off, and six hours of sleep for me is the equivalent of about 30 minutes for the average person. I was awakened from my fitful slumber by sounds of shuffling and clunking mere inches from my head. When I opened my eyes, my field of vision was virtually consumed by Barry's tawny head. He was already hard at work removing the heater. Barry's hair is quite voluminous and unruly anyway, and, unkempt as it was after a night of sleep, I thought for a moment I was staring up the ass of a bull elk.

Ricky was a bit groggy, but he revived quickly as we brought him down through the thermoclines. His general disposition in the morning is not unlike someone in the first stages of carbon monoxide poisoning anyway. I straddled Barry and began frying eggs and bacon while he explained his nocturnal revelation to no one in particular.

"The striker," he explained, "needs to be readjusted to compensate for the thin mountain air. Remember how we used to have to change the jets in the carburetors of our motorcycles when we brought them up here? It's the same principle."

"Jets?" drawled Les. "You guys are nuts!"

Barry decided to take the heating unit to the bed of his truck where he had more elbowroom to work. The prospect of being out in the sun was attractive to us all, and we watched as he dismantled the heater down to its bare bones. This is classic shade-tree approach to mechanics. I had seen my dad do it hundreds of times. If you take something apart and put it back together, you have about a 50-50 chance that it will work even if the would be mechanic does not know exactly why. I figure about 90% of all mechanical work is based on this principle. Then again, I've heard that 75% of all statistics are made up on the spot, so it's hard to say.

I noticed right off that Barry's shade-tree manner was quite different from that of my dad. Dad's involved a lot of bleeding, pinching, and smashing of appendages along with the requisite swearing. Uncooperative parts and tools were apt to take flight on wings of fury. One of my jobs was to find small washers, nuts, and screws when they landed in the dense undergrowth of Mom's garden. Fortunately, with the shade-tree approach, you always wind up with a few "extra" parts left over, which helped compensate for the loss. I must admit, Barry's patient approach struck me as being far too calm and orderly to result in any real success. He was not teaching the stubborn heater any lessons about who was boss. From watching Dad, I had come to believe that the secret to these kinds of enterprises involved establishing authority over the inanimate object through verbal humiliation and rough handling. "That's the only way they'll learn," his actions seemed to say.

What is more, Barry was too comfortable. No respectable mechanic in Dad's world ever moved what he was working on so that the job would be easier. Dad liked to work on his back, looking up, so that any dirt that got dislodged would fall into his eyes, resulting in a reflex jerk that would bring his head in contact with the nearest well anchored piece of metal. If possible, he parked his vehicles over a bed of sharp gravel when they needed maintenance. Hot asphalt is a good second choice in the summer, especially if it is bubbling and sticky. Plus, you've got to get into some contorted position that will bring on multiple muscle cramps. It's best if you crawl under on your stomach, and then roll over, but only with the upper half of your body, wedging your shoulder under the exhaust pipe, which, of course, must be scorching hot. Only pansies work on a cool engine.

Barry's attempt to get comfortable met with a reaction from the weather, in keeping with the first law of camping dynamics. A thin layer of clouds blew in to cover the sun and keep the temperature from getting way up in the 20s. We were even graced with a light dusting of snow. Barry was undaunted, and in a couple of hours he had made the proper adjustments in accordance with his dream, and reassembled the heater. Then it was back to the kitchen floor for yet another test run. By this time, we were becoming proficient in our roles with respect to this procedure. Barry reinstalled the heater, which fired up without hesitation and gave us the first warm air we had felt in 12 hours—for about 45 seconds, then it quit again.

I have lost track of how many solutions Barry has devised and dreamed over the intervening years. I can testify that removing and reinstalling the heater has become part of our camping routine—it has never worked. Yet, every year, I get a call from Ol' Barry the day after we return.

"You will never guess where I am," he begins.

I play along, "You're in Nairobi looking for flank feathers from a pygmy ostrich for some 'can't miss' fly pattern?"

"No," he snickers. "I am in the camper in front of my house. The heater is running and it is toasty warm in here!"

Yet the Pain In the Ass Quotient remains constant.

Murphy Goes Camping

Chapter 13

Let There Be Light....Please?

Campers can be an irritable lot. The reason is simple. We are trying to escape months of pent up frustration by cramming more fun than is possible into a very small window of time. Nothing interfering with this goal will be received well. I have taken it upon myself to compose a top ten list, à la David Letterman, of actions sure to arouse the ire of the typical camping enthusiast. You may find this useful either in avoiding said anger or in determining what offenses might merit retaliation.

Top Ten Ways to Annoy Your Fellow Campers

10) Driving though a campground designated for units 12 feet and under in a 45-foot RV that costs more than the combined value of all the homes of all the campers currently ogling you. (Suggested response: "Why don't you just buy your own national park?")

9) Driving through the same campground in that same RV while towing a Hummer.

8) Warming up a diesel truck before five a.m. (This is common among elk hunters who seem proud of the fact that their hobby is more miserable than your job.)

7) Taking a family of more than two generations swimming in the special trout water.

6) Relieving yourself outside within 100 yards of the facilities during the daytime. (This is allowed at night though doing so while carrying on a conversation is frowned upon by those whose temperaments are more refined.)

5) Roaring your matching four-wheelers past hikers so you can swim in the special trout water that they have been walking toward for three days. (WARNING: Though it seems physically impossible, four-wheelers have been known to kick up rocks that somehow hit such riders in the back of the head.)

4) Camping with yipping dogs that have delusions of grandeur and no sporting value. (Rule of thumb: Don't bring a dog so small that it only whets a bear's appetite for domesticated flesh. It should take a mountain lion at least one minute to eat your dog so that I have time to get away.)

3) Cleaning your trout under the community water spigot.

2) Dressing out an elk under the community spigot while cooling down your diesel truck.

1) Butchering Bambi on or near the camp playground, though this may be done discreetly at naptime.

The camping aficionado who has any experience at all is likely to notice a glaring omission in this list. There are those who would claim that the most obnoxious and irritating behavior engaged in at a campground is the use of the gas-powered generator. It seems to me, however, that one's opinion on this matter depends on his or her vantage point. Those on the receiving end of the electricity provided by the generator have developed long and twisted rationalizations for their behavior. Those who do not benefit, but must endure the noise, have long and twisted fantasies about where the owner might store this obnoxious machine. The reason I did not include this on my list is…well, let's just say that this story is a confession of sorts, and it is with great trepidation that I enter into it. As someone who has experienced the generator from both perspectives, I feel compelled to attempt to bring peace between these factions through civil discourse.

Let me begin my explanation by assuring you that, in my mountain man days, I was an avowed opponent of all things motorized. I was a camper of the old code. The only form of light that any self-respecting camper could employ was the campfire. It provides no usable light, no consistent warmth, a high smoke-to-heat ratio, is difficult to get going, and difficult to put out. All these potential frustrations, along with the illusory promise of comfort, made it the hands-down favorite among campers.

When a traditional campfire is not possible, due to restrictions or a lack of harvestable fuel, one may resort to the gas-powered lantern.

Apparently, up until the autumn of 1871, when Mrs.

O'Leary's cow scratched an itch that lit up Chicago, no one questioned the wisdom of a flame existing usefully and safely within four inches of its fuel source. Ironically, this was the precise moment that the lantern became popular among outdoor enthusiasts. They realized that this device could be as dangerous and as frustrating as the campfire when used correctly. The oil lamp, however, proved to be far too easy to master. The hardy and well-seasoned campers foresaw that this improvement would likely attract a cumbersome number of soft-handed butterbeans to the great outdoors. As keepers of the camping flame, they must have felt that the oil lamp needed some modifications that would discourage the comfortable. Enter Mr. Coleman.

The first step involved was compressing the fuel to increase volatility, creating the potential for explosion. Then, there was developed a means of delivering this gas to a magical little piece of cloth, which, like Moses' burning bush, was aflame, but not consumed. This little cloth is referred to as the "mantle." If this term sounds a bit foreign to you, welcome to the world of Coleman. Included in the parts list of typical lantern, you will find the following: a ventilator, a generator, a fount assembly, a cleaner stem assembly, a check valve, a pump plunger assembly, a bail, and, my personal favorite, the eccentric block (not to be confused with a neighborhood composed of odd people). Clearly, the reasoning was that anyone not put off by the threat of explosion might be discouraged by sheer complexity. An equally compelling theory holds that the modern lantern was the product of scientists and engineers, dedicated to making the simple more complex, who became bored between the completion of the atomic bomb and the space race.

No one I know, including those who can use one quite well, really understands how the gas lantern works. Not since the utterance of the immortal words, "Let there be light," has such a mysterious mode of illumination been created, and it has been my experience that only those born before 1950 can get much out of them. From the get-go, the art seems to be fraught with complex, often self-contradicting demands. For instance, the mantle cannot be touched under any circumstances and must be burned before it can be used—the classic Catch-22.

Legend has it that the first lanterns of this type produced by Mr. Coleman included instructions. After a few chosen people learned to use the lantern, however, written instructions were dispensed with so that only the initiated could pass on the art, resulting in even tighter control over who could benefit from the advancement. No self-respecting camper would be caught dead reading instructions anyway, since they tend to lower the PIAQ—at least when they are written in English. The accepted method, therefore, of learning the secrets of the lantern is received by tradition, passed on by a father, or at least a father figure, in a manner reminiscent of the passing on of treasured Eastern customs:

"Hand me the mantle, young Ash-wipe," says the master—Dad was mine, of course. Ash-wipe is the title of the initiate who has been apprenticing by tending the campfire.

"Pardon, Sensei?" I respond. "I know not what you refer to. There is no fireplace here."

"Uncross the eyes of your mind, little one," says the master. "The mantle is the small white mesh bag before you."

At this point I reach for the bag, but am stopped short with a lightning quick karate chop to the forearm and a stern reprimand, "NO, Ash -wipe. You must never touch the mantle!"

"Hand it to you, but do not touch it?" I ask. "Ash-wipe is confused, oh, Brightened One."

"Oil from fingers fouls the cloth," says the master, smiling.

This phrase is to be taken both literally and figuratively as a deep proverb among the illuminated. "You can never touch the mantle. Handle it only by the strings. This is the First Great Truth."

"I see! Please continue, oh Lit-up One." I bow.

"The unburned mantle will not light," explains the master. "This is the Second Great Truth." Again, the meaning is multi-layered.

"How can that which has never been burned, and thus cannot be lit, ever be lit seeing that it must first be burned?" I respond. "Can a man begin a journey before he has taken a step? Can a man take a step without beginning a journey? Surely these things are too deep for me, oh Well-Seasoned One!"

"If you cannot untangle the cords of your mind, little Sooty and Soiled One, you will forever wipe the ash of another," sighs the master. Roughly translated, this means pull your head out. "Just as the egg precedes the chicken, but the chicken lays the egg, so it is with the mantle. One cannot use it in the lantern until one has burned it."

"But how can one use it after it is burned, oh Dry and Flaky One?" I continue.

"Witness the miracle of the mantle, my child!" responds the master.

As he held it gingerly by the drawstring, Dad proceeded to light a match that he then held beneath the mantle. The effect was quite fascinating. The mantle actually burns until it appears to be nothing but white ash. Yet, unless it has been touched by some careless ash-wipe, it remains intact. Then, and only then, is it ready to be used in the lantern. Unfortunately for Dad, the initial pre-ash flame of the burning mantle danced ominously close to his fingers.

I made one last observation before the Eastern mystique was doused in a flood of Western expletives, "Pray, is the cuff of your down jacket supposed to be aflame, oh Illuminated One?"

As for the rest of the process, all I can tell you is that it involves a complex pumping action that requires a level of digital coordination that is truly awe-inspiring. Most of us, when allowed to try, either will get a weak flame from the mythical mantle or produce the classic flame out. This occurs when the fire escapes not only the mantle, but also the confines of the glass housing itself. At this point, the lantern bearer will typically resort to the Coleman Strut, which is somewhat like a foxtrot with a pyrotechnic element added.

Unfortunately, it was evident from the start that I was among the "lantern challenged." This is a grave indictment in camping circles. If no remedy is found, such a person bears a great deal of shame. His lantern is taken in an act carried out with the same attitude that a disgraced soldier's stripes are ripped from his arm, and he is given a battery-powered lantern with fluorescent bulbs as a token of humiliation. His teacher then ceremonially washes his hands, signifying that the initiate is now beyond illumination. He then lights the lantern he has taken, and over-pressurizes it until it becomes so bright that the initiate is forced to cover his eyes and retreat into the shadows, where he will live out the rest of his camping days among the artificially illuminated.

When it comes to light, the campfire and the lantern have one thing in common; they both produce what might appropriately be called one-dimensional light. I am not a scientist, so I cannot explain the physics of this type of light. The effect, however, is that it lights up only one side of an object at any given moment—one plane out of the three we are used to viewing life in. You feel somewhat like a cartoon character living in a flat world.

I am a night owl by nature, and one-dimensional light is simply not adequate for most of what I need to do. Typically, by dark, I leave the river convinced of one of two truths. Either there is some obscure fly pattern, which, had I been carrying it, would have made this day one for the annals. Or, alternatively, that there is a technical flaw, probably a microscopic one, which, if addressed, would turn half a dozen ten-inch trout into a dozen and a half 18-inch trout.

The remedy to both of these possibilities, I have learned from experience, will require a decent light source, for I will either need to tie up a few of these obscure patterns, in at least two shades and four sizes, or I will need to research a solution from my vast portable library of fly-fishing documents. This library, naturally, is a carefully selected condensation of the vastly larger library I have at home. The home library is a product of years of careful observation and collection of all the most important works on fly-fishing from Izaak Walton to Gary Borger, with a dose of Tappley and Macmanus thrown in for balance.

This library, and my devotion to it, has made me the target of quite a bit of ridicule over the years, but let us remember what the preacher of Ecclesiastes had to say:

"The words of wise men are like goads, and masters of these collections are like well-driven nails." That's me—a master collector. Okay, I'll admit that is not the end of his thoughts on the matter, "But beyond this, my son, be warned: of the making of books there is no end, and much study doth weary the bones." (Eccl. 12:11-12)

So, I am a master collector with weary bones.

"How many fish have you caught out of that book?" My

dad would often ask. Maybe I do spend more time preparing to fish than I do fishing, but isn't that just the nature of the fly-fishing beast? Besides, I'm living in the moment, enjoying both the preparation and the execution, and I cannot be blamed if jealous observers want to expend themselves mocking me. The clever ones can be quite entertaining, anyway.

Barry and I were once dissecting some river insects and comparing them to the examples from a 300 page entomology textbook we happened to have with us. (Actually, this was the abridged streamside companion edition of a six volume exhaustive concordance that we did not have room to carry.) At that moment, Brian commented, "Do you guys ever get around to actually fishing, or are you just out to master bait?"

Chapter 14

The Night Genny Got the Clap

The need to tie flies and carry out prudent literary investigations is what finally pushed Barry and I over the edge and landed us in the world of portable generators. It was not a proud moment, and was met with great angst. The shattered tranquility of the campground, the stares, the muttered epithets, not to mention the oblique hand signals, were things we had convinced ourselves we were prepared to endure as due and just punishment for our luxurious excess. Our greatest fear was the possibility of outright, face-to-face conflict. We tend to make monsters out of anything we do not understand, and Barry and I had this attitude toward conflict.

The polite Southern sensibility that reigned in Gruver during our formative years had taught us that conflict resolution was something one never dealt with in a straightforward manner. The proper course, when offended, was to share the matter with as many people as possible, but never directly with the offending party.

This approach has two benefits. First, it allows the victim to hone his or her story surrounding the offense to best suit the case against the offender in venues where he or she will not be challenged. That way, when the grapevine brings news of the matter back around to the original offender, any details that have survived are blurred so that the ensuing argument can be purely personal right from the start. Second, it gives the victim time to work up a head of steam and blow the matter completely out of proportion. Without this emotional buildup, the victim will likely find themselves in a reasonable frame of mind when the chips are down—handicapping his or her ability to launch an effective personal assault against the perpetrator.

Another Southern sensibility, honor, meant that if a conflict ever reached the face-to-face stage, and was properly cast as personal, things would likely get physical. This conclusion was based largely on anecdotal evidence. This evidence was skewed somewhat, however, since the only face-to-face conflicts we witnessed usually involved the town grouch.

Small Southern communities typically have at least one male citizen who has achieved a state of perpetual disgruntlement. He spends most of his life collecting grudges, which, in time, pile up as chips on his shoulders. In fact, he becomes so adept at taking offense that he soon accumulates more than he can keep track of. Not only does he forget the details of the specific incidents that have put him at odds with "so and so," he eventually loses track of whom exactly he is at odds with at any given time. To cover his bases, he finally treats everyone in town as if they have personally offended him. This makes him a popular sideshow at little league baseball games where he is prone to fly off the handle and get into a row with an umpire, another fan, a coach, a third-grade shortstop, or some teenage concession stand attendant. In our young minds, we made a permanent association between conflict and assault, and carefully avoided the former for fear of the latter.

Naturally, this approach to conflict begs the classic question made famous by Dr. Phil, "And how's that working for you?" I fear that demographic studies of his most interesting guests, as well as those of Jerry Springer, might reveal that they tend to come from communities that are too familiar to those of us who grew up in the Texas Panhandle.

On this particular trip, Barry and I were into our third night of generator use, and were scrupulously adhering to the posted restrictions, "The use of gas-powered generators is prohibited between the hours of 10 p.m. and 8 a.m." Our shame with respect to this matter was heightened by the fact that neither of us could remember ever noticing this posted restriction before we started bringing Genny, as we affectionately called her, which made us wonder if we were not the sole reason for the notice.

Genny was a hand-me-down from my dad. Of course, as a Lantern Master of the 32nd degree, he never used it camping, only to power his compressor and paint sprayer. This was not one of those newfangled, whisper-quiet units on which you can hang

165

a hummingbird feeder. This was a man's generator, like Tim the Toolman might own. On the job site, extra decibels are actually a source of pride. You lose less productivity through chatting and you can make it sound like you are getting a lot more done than you really are. In place of a muffler, Genny must have had some kind of amplifier.

Originally, Genny came along strictly as a backup in case Barry's camper batteries happened to run low. According to the manufacturer, this was rarely—if ever—going to happen. Of course, retailers do not understand the constancy of the PIAQ. The system is set up so that the batteries charge while en route. For us, that was an eight hour trip, which sounded like more than enough time to get the batteries up to peak potential. The RV battery is designed to charge fast and provide virtually indefinite deep cycle power, in theory. Of course, in theory, we had central heat, too! On paper, if you do the math—Barry has—two hours of charging from the alternator of a Ford Cummins 350 diesel running at 2,000 rpms should provide enough electricity to light Times Square for roughly three weeks. In fact, our experience taught us that two hours of charging gets you about 30 minutes of good burn time if you are careful. That meant restricting ourselves to the use of a single 75 watt bulb, and opening the refrigerator only in emergencies, since it cost us five minutes of light.

On this occasion, we had intended to give Genny a night off, sparing the rest of the campers the noise. However, we discovered that we had somehow arrived without a single egg-sucking leech between the two of us! This is a crisis of dire proportions, as any fly-fisherman worth his salt will attest, since the ESL is the MasterCard of flies—you don't leave home with it! To wet a boot without at least a couple of egg-sucking leeches in reserve is just bad form.

In all honesty, neither of us has ever had much luck with the pattern, except once when we found some pond-bound trout that had been stocked too thick and were starving. Nevertheless, every year, when our favorite fly-fishing magazine ran its perennial article on "Ten Flies You Don't Want to be Without," the egg-sucking leech was always somewhere near the top of the list. Most of the other flies would change from year to year, and that always made me wonder if the articles were more of a marketing gimmick than sound information. However, there was never any doubt about the ESL. Just to drive home the point, at least one magazine cover per year had a close-up of a huge brown trout with an ESL hanging out of the corner of his gaping jaw.

Furthermore, during a frustrating lull in the afternoon's action on the river, I had remembered an article from that publication that had something to do with putting action in a nymph through the judicious use of the pinky finger, above the last knuckle, on the fly-fisherman's line hand. This technique was picked up by the American contingency at the 1999 International Fly-Fishing Championship. Apparently, the team from Uzbekistan had thoroughly trounced our boys, and investigation revealed that the pinky twitch was their secret weapon. Barry and I discussed the matter and determined that it would be nothing short of irresponsible for us to hit the river the next day without a couple of egg-sucking leeches, while having the mechanics of the Uzbekistan twitch fresh on our minds.

In hindsight, we realized that we could have spared ourselves the shameful humiliation we were about to experience if we had simply shared our airtight reasoning on this matter with our fellow campers, but our polite Southern sensibilities demanded that we not risk disturbing our neighbors with conversation, so we gritted our teeth and fired up Genny.

During our justification discussion, we had convinced ourselves that what we heard as noise probably only registered as a quiet hum to everyone but us because of our proximity to the source. We were sure that generators, like kids, always sound louder to their owners than to anyone else around.

"It's really not that loud," I screamed as the generator roared to life. "I'll bet they don't even notice it over there!"

"What?" responded Barry. "You say there's a hatch going on in my hair?"

I thought I heard something about "throwing down with a bear," and led a hasty retreat back into the camper.

We tied furiously until precisely 9:58 p.m., at which time Barry promptly shut down the generator. We wanted to be good sports and ere on the side of caution regarding the posted restrictions. When Barry returned to the camper, I noticed he was a bit pale.

"Did you hear that?" he asked

"No," I said. "My ears are ringing a little…from the altitude, no doubt."

"As soon as I shut Genny down," Barry whispered—at least it sounded like whispering to me—"the guy over at site 23 started clapping!"

"Clapping?" I repeated.

"Yeh," said Barry. "You know, like he was applauding the fact that we finally shut down the generator."

Shame and fear settled in on us, thick as an early summer caddis hatch. There was only one way to interpret such an action. We had just become the recipients of the classic smart-ass response. In small Southern communities, the smart-ass response is a precursor to direct confrontation that leads to an "ass-whuppin." The smart-ass response is the Southern equivalent of an

Englishman being slapped with a glove as a challenge to duel.

The only honorable response would be for us to escalate the matter with an equally smart-ass retort, "Thank you. Our next performance will begin at five a.m. For advanced seating, you can come kiss my ass!" But we felt ourselves above such childish playground antics. Okay, maybe we were more interested in protecting our asses than our honor.

Unfortunately, failure to respond to such an insult is no guarantee that the matter is over. In fact, failure to respond telegraphs weakness and often emboldens the smart-ass. If he was wise, he likely sized us up prior to his affront, and must have concluded that he had enough support in his company to meet any resistance we were bold enough to offer, which was very little. We secured the plastic bolt-lock on the camper door, and began to think out loud.

"Perhaps a posse is being formed even as we cower! What might they do? Sabotage? Intimidation? Battery?" Battery would be poetic punishment. Maybe they would go after Genny instead of us! Our imaginations got the best of us as the camper lights faded. Barry tried to tie another leech while I read the article detailing the Uzbekistan twitch, but neither of us was able to bring our attention to bear on these critical matters for wondering what might be developing outside the relative safety of the camper.

Tying flies has a tranquilizing effect on Barry. As soon as he picks up his scissors, his eyelids droop. This, coupled with his carpenter's manicure that shreds material on contact, has resulted in some interesting patterns over the years, including the Phyllis Diller, The Angry Pa, Bad Hair Day, Don King, and his all-time favorite, the Red Ribbed Wooly Bugger, also known as the Menstruating Leech. This night, with the stress of the impending conflict working on him, he did not last long. Since stress has the opposite effect on me, I stayed up, taking the first watch. For supplemental light, I turned to my battery powered, fluorescent pseudolantern—the lamp of shame—and continued to tie, alert for any possible signs of foul play.

As usual, Barry was dreaming before his head even hit the pillow. Cleary, the generator matter and its potential fallout were still torturing him, and the things he muttered in is sleep did not ease my worried mind in the least. "You sure have a purdy mouth," he mumbled.

It must have been about 2:00 a.m. when I put the whip finish on my final leech and grabbed a flashlight for one last trip to the facilities before hitting the sack. It had been several hours since the clapping incident and I was certain that we had worked ourselves into a panic over nothing, as it did not appear that the occupant of site 23 had any plans of adding injury to his insult. By this time, I was much more concerned about the possibility of running into a marauding bear as my course took me by the very same dumpsters where we had discovered a trapped bear a couple of years back.

Barry had not stirred since about an hour earlier when he made a sound that was all too reminiscent of a squealing pig. I unfastened the plastic bolt and slipped out into the night, dancing my flashlight beam into the trees as I made my way across the campground. I'm not sure what that accomplishes, except that I might catch a glimpse of my attacker that would give me time to soil myself before I was eaten. (Would that make me more or less palatable to a bear?) I was also making hushed conversation with any wildlife that might be lurking in the shadows. I had read that bears don't like to be surprised, and neither do I, for that matter. As usual, the walk was uneventful.

Meanwhile back at the camper, Barry had been rudely

awakened by a bladder spasm that commonly strikes middle-aged men at least once every night, more often, it seems, if bathroom facilities are not conveniently nearby. Assuming I was fast asleep in my cubbyhole at the far end of the camper, he snuck out, dressed only in his tighty-whitie briefs. He did not even bother to don his shoes, so urgent was the call. He did not intend to trek all the way to the outhouse.

Having concluded my business post haste, as is my custom when the temperature of the toilet seat is below 35 degrees, I was making my way back to the camper, still playing my light into the trees and carrying on casual banter. Barry had gone only about 30 feet from the camper and while in the midst of relieving himself, he noticed that someone with a flashlight was walking toward our camper. What's more, he could hear them muttering in hushed tones.

More than one person on a midnight stroll through an otherwise darkened campground could mean only one thing: "Revenge of the clapper!" Dreams of *Deliverance* still fresh on his mind, he stopped mid-flow, not an easy thing for a middle aged man to do, collected himself, and made a dash for the camper door. In his haste, he forgot that our shade awning was extended and the aluminum brace caught him square across the forehead.

I was beginning to think I was home free when the racket of his collision reached me. Since I was approaching from the opposite side of the camper, I could not see what was transpiring. I froze, imagining the worst, "A bear…in our campsite; The Revenge of Cimarron."

Meanwhile, Barry recovered and stumbled the last few feet to the camper. He weighs well over 200 pounds, and the rap to the noggin, along with tender bare feet, put a shuffle in his gate that made him sound all too much like what I imagined him to be.

He must have just pulled the door closed when I peaked around the corner and saw…nothing!

"Of course," I thought "It's the bear you can't see that gets you!" Hadn't I read that somewhere? I was only 15 feet from the door, and the relative safety of the camper, at this point. "If I could just make it inside and engage that plastic bolt!" I thought.

Barry had stopped just inside the camper door and was watching in horror as the flashlight beam came around the corner of the camper and moved right toward our door, which he had not latched. His reasoning, perhaps still influenced by the knock on the head, was that our assailant would surely hear the latch close, thus robbing him of his only advantage—that of surprise.

As I reached the door, I noticed it was unlatched and slightly ajar. This was a disturbing discovery as I was certain I had closed it securely when I left. Up until this point, my hope lay in the fact that the bear was without, and I was but a step from being within. My body was still operating on this assumption as I reached for the handle, but my brain was already formulating another possibility, "I wonder if that bear could have gotten inside the camper!"

For a brief moment, two alternate realities became tangled in my mind. I was being charged from behind by one bear while diving right into the claws of another! Reflex won out, however, and my body followed through on my original plan. My arm eased the door open, and my legs flexed for what would have been my leap to safety or certain death.

In the short time Barry had to formulate his defense, he had decided to stand just inside the door and scream "Bwaaaaoooooo!" when the culprits made their move. I cannot say whether this would have disoriented the would-be attackers, but I can tell you that, for someone who is expecting a bear, it is a very effective maneuver!

My limbs responded involuntarily, each trying to run off in its own direction, before giving out altogether, while my brain tried in vain to process the baffling appearance of what could only be a 6' 4", albino black bear dressed in neon white underwear. All Barry saw was the wild light display created by my flailing flashlight, which gave the illusion that he was facing at least three lightning quick ninja warriors who were falling into attack formation.

I rattled off six of the eight bear insults I had prepared before we both realized, simultaneously, what had just happened. I cannot help but think that there was some sort of karma at work in this incident. It had to be some a divinely orchestrated event meant to chasten us for disturbing the tranquility of God's forest with our generator. I don't see how this could have transpired as it did purely by chance. And to the camper in site 23, let me assure you that you could not have devised a sweeter revenge.

EPILOGUE

The morning after Genny got the clap, Barry and I decided she could do with some time off and chose not to fire her up. Like the thin film of frost on Barry's windshield, our fear had melted with the first rays of the morning sun. In fact, we decided we should bug out early for waters more remote rather than risk an encounter with the mysterious "Clapper." We agreed that this was in his best interest. After all, we did not want to be backed into a corner and hence forced to hurt someone. Barry had also taken advantage of the light to rummage through his camper tool stash and retrieve Sluggo, just in case.

Feeling reasonably secure in the cab of Barry's F-450, we decided to swing by camp site 23 to see if we could catch a glimpse of our foe. Much to our surprise, the site was empty. Though I had been up quite late, and Barry had arisen very early, neither of us had heard any vehicles coming or going from the campground. It was as if our antagonist had vanished into thin air.

As we exited the truck to investigate, I had a sudden realization, "You know, this was the last camping spot Dean ever occupied."

"You're right," Barry said. "Kind of freaky, isn't it? Hey, look at this." He picked up something from the picnic table and held it between his thumb and forefinger.

A chill went up my spine. "That looks like…" I began as he handed it to me, and I brought it to my nose.

"A Swisher Sweet?" Barry gasped.

"Yeh," I put the butt of the cigar, well chewed and damp from the morning dew, back on the picnic table, handling it as one might handle some precious religious artifact.

"Warren!" Barry whispered. "Look at the fire pit!"

There, among the otherwise ashen refuse of what had been someone's camping goodies, stood a 44-ounce Styrofoam cup of the type that had surely held a fountain drink. I stared in disbelief. "Dean never left home without one."

"Yeh, and check this out." Barry stirred through the ashes, uncovering a couple of tins. There was enough of a label left to see that the taller of the two had been a can of shoestring potatoes, the same brand Dean packed aboard the S.S. Livin' each trip. We did not need a label to identify the second since its shape was well-known to both of us. It was a sardine tin.

Without another word, we backed reverently from the site, climbed into the truck and eased out of the campground, anxious to put a little distance between ourselves and site 23 with its mysteriously familiar contents.

For years before Dean passed away, I battled, yet dared not give voice to, crippling thoughts about what it might be like to return to paradise without him. I guess I thought that maybe paradise, for me, would die with him. Maybe my mind, by association, would make a hell of that heaven. I suppose I was engaging in my own brand of PISD, sometimes sinking neck deep in the grief of what might have been.

As site 23 disappeared from the site of our rearview mirror that day, fully five years after Dean's death, I realized that I had worried, yet again, in vain. The truth is, and I think I can speak for the entire Brotherhood, there will never really be any such thing as camping without Dean. He is always there.

In fact, sometimes "Ol' Barry" and I wonder if Dean has not cut a deal with the man upstairs—who has a history of partiality toward fishermen, after all—that allows him to throw a wrench in the works now and then just to let us know he's still around. Bull-bear calls, faint and distant, sometimes reach our ears as we trudge along some mountain trail in the dark. Scratching and grunting sounds are occasionally heard emanating from the vicinity of trash dumpsters late at night. Barry, who was once quite sure-footed astream, insists that someone or something is moving rocks around under his feet. When he scrambles for his balance, he claims adamantly that the same slick wobbly rock will appear wherever he chooses to step next.

Sometimes I even catch fleeting glimpses of Dean in my own reflection, or in the profile of one of my brothers, as we all creep inevitably through middle age. But he is most present in those moments when things go awry. For instance, when the outboard motor stalls or when a washboard road dumps a 44-ounce fountain drink in my lap. At the times when I accidentally pierce my ear with a weighted Wooly Bugger or realize I only packed one leg of my hip waders, or when I sacrifice yet another rod tip to a car door or when the first quart of icy stream water breaches the top of my waders to numb my toes.

I know that, in some way, Dean is there in those moments, and that he is enjoying my frustration with a chuckle or two, as only a seasoned camper could. When I lose a fish, I often hear a whisper in the wind, which seems to be saying, "I told you not to horse 'im!" When I climb a tree to retrieve a fly, or sit on the bank dissecting a hopeless tangle of leader material, the gurgles around my feet will sometime chide me in a familiar tone, "Warren, I read that 99% of all trout are IN the water."

Dad handed down his legacy so naturally and effortlessly

that he was really unaware he was doing it. The best of legacies typically are passed on this way. Strangely enough, it was "Ol' Barry," not usually known for his sensitivity, who first put his finger on it. He stopped by the hospital on his way to Colorado where he planned to test his iron will against the sales pressure of a timeshare outfit, bragging that he was going to bilk them out of a free vacation since there was "no way" they could reel him in. (Of course, I got an "Ol' Barry" call within the week that started, "You will never believe they deal I got!"). The timing of the visit ended up being one of Dean's final days.

During a conversation with my mom at the hospital, Barry stated what we all felt concerning Dean's legacy: "You know, when I think about the impact Dean had on our family, and about all the people he introduced to the Rocky Mountains…" Barry, overcome by emotion, was unable to finish.

That sentence still hangs in the air, as well it should. The tribute and the legacy flow on, like the rivers to which Dean led us, over the boots and hearts of succeeding generations of those who share his love of the Rocky Mountains and cherish the fellowship of others thus smitten. To us, the water sings, and it was Dean who gave the melody its lyrics, capturing the soul of the matter with characteristic brevity:

"Now boys, this is 'Livin'!"

www.warrenmcclenagan.com

TAG Publishing, LLC
2618 S. Lipscomb
Amarillo, TX 79109
806.373.0114
806.373.4004 fax

www.TAGPublishers.com

Contact us at: info@TAGPublishers.com

Reel **LIVIN'**

www.ingramcontent.com/pod-product-compliance
Lightning Source LLC
Chambersburg PA
CBHW052003090426
42741CB00008B/1528